HOMEMADE
CHEESE

Recipes for
50 Cheeses
from Artisan
Cheesemakers

Janet Hurst

Voyageur Press

Dedication

Dedicated to my family: Jamie, Charlie, my mother, and my late father. Thank you for believing in me, for milking a goat now and then, and for tasting lots of cheese.

First published in 2011 by Voyageur Press, an imprint of MBI Publishing Company, 400 First Avenue North, Suite 300, Minneapolis, MN 55401 USA

Copyright © 2011 by Janet Hurst

Photographs on pages 31, 82, 90, 105, 117, 122, 124, 138, 143, and 146 by Paul Markert. Other photographs by the author and from Shutterstock.

Voyageur Press titles are also available at discounts in bulk quantity for industrial or sales-promotional use. For details write to Special Sales Manager at MBI Publishing Company, 400 First Avenue North, Suite 300, Minneapolis, MN 55401 USA.

To find out more about our books, visit us online at www.voyageurpress.com.

ISBN-13: 978-0-7603-3848-3

Editor: Michael Dregni

Design Manager: Katie Sonmor

Layout by: Sandra Salamony

Designed by: Ellen Huber and Sandra Salamony

Cover designed by: Ellen Huber

Printed in China

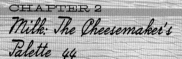

CONTENTS

INTRODUCTION

In the beginning, there was a goat, and it was good. The goat—a marauder, escape artist, and con man—ate the garden, and it was not good. Such is life and the beginning of my journey: life with goats. I look back and wonder, sometimes, how it all began.

Growing up in the middle of Hannibal, Missouri, on one of the busiest streets in town, I lived for the weekends. On Saturday mornings, my family headed for a river camp where we fished, swam, and enjoyed life to the fullest. Dinner was caught straight out of the river, vegetables cooked from the garden out back. Life was easy and free. Heaven waited for us on the banks of the old muddy Mississippi. If we weren't at the river, then we would venture out to my great grandmother's farm. I fondly remember trips to the hen house to collect eggs; bringing in water, cold and fresh from the well; even trips to the outhouse, guarded by a threatening rooster. These all remain as snapshots of my youth. I waded in the creek, picked apples ripe from the tree, rang the old dinner bell, and found kittens in the hay loft. It was a little girl's paradise. The proverbial seed was planted.

Years later, as a young mother myself, I began to dream of a piece of land—a small farm where I could raise my son and share the wonders of rural living with him. Eventually we found such a place: a few acres, a little creek, a place to call our own. We began to take root.

Gardens were planted, chickens purchased, and eggs hatched. We learned a lot—most of it the hard way. Things looked a lot easier at Great Grandma's house. I found there was a whole new language to learn, distinct verbiage attached to each endeavor: queen bees, worker bees, drones, fungicides, pullets, layers, straight runs, laying mash, oyster shells, scratch grains—the list went on and on. Behind each new word there were important details awaiting discovery by the greenhorn, wannabe farmer. We had all the experiences one would expect and many we could not have imagined: chickens that drowned, rabbits who refused to mate, dogs that ran away, cats who didn't. Some days it was paradise; other days a nightmare. We persevered.

I read—book after book describing the good life and how to get it. We learned we could build with stone and eat from wooden bowls, dig a cellar by hand, grow our own wheat and make our own bread—from scratch, literally. I read all the books, magazines, and papers extolling

Goats arrive early in the morning for their daily milking.

the romantic views of country living. I went after it full force, grew a garden to feed the masses, then pickled, fermented, dried, and canned until the pantry could not contain the stores. Only one thing was missing: a goat.

As I read back through the maga zines of the 1970s, especially *Mother Earth News* and *Countryside*, it seems everyone had a Volkswagen, a backpack, and a goat. Without fail, the goats were always smiling, happy-looking creatures, and I decided country life could not possibly be complete without one. Or two. Everyone I knew tried to talk me out of it. My parents shook their heads and wondered where they had gone wrong. After all, I had been raised to be a "proper lady," not one wearing overalls and gum boots.

I found my prince one day at a flea market. I pulled money from my well-worn backpack and paid for the rights of ownership for my first goat—a billy, at that. I tucked him in the back of my Volkswagen bug. He was handsome, a young Nubian buck. I was in love. I named him Amos.

A selection of cheeses that can be easily made in your own home, from simple farmhouse goat cheese to a blue Stilton.

One goat is a lonely goat. Amos cried for companions and girlfriends. I complied with his wishes and purchased an Alpine nanny, in full milk. I named her Dolly Parton for two obvious reasons.

Now, there are lessons to be learned in the goat world. Lesson number one: a nanny sold in full milk is sold for a reason. Nobody is going to raise a goat, feed it all winter, and then sell her when she is in milk unless there is a pretty good reason. There was. Dolly Parton had horrible milk. This being my first goat, I didn't know any better and secretly wondered why everyone was so excited about this milk that tasted so terrible. One thing Dolly was good for was volume. She made lots of horrible milk, bless her soul. I decided to make cheese from it. Lesson number two: horrible milk makes horrible cheese.

I was not to be beaten, so I bought another goat. She gave the best milk I have ever had. It was rich, full of cream. She was another Nubian, the same breed as

Billy Goat Likes to Butt His Head

Would you believe out of all my childhood artwork, this is the piece my mother saved? I must have known even back then what colorful creatures goats were. Believe me, truer words were never spoken than "Billy goat likes to butt his head!"

My son, Jamie, as a budding gardener in 1987. Jamie grew up with goats as companions, sometimes having to share the back seat of the car with them. The values he learned on the farm have stayed with him always.

Amos. She had long, bassett hound–looking ears, a Roman nose, and an udder that swayed seductively back and forth as she pranced through the pasture. No wonder Amos was smitten. His behavior changed the day this lovely creature cycled through her first heat. Amos turned from mild-mannered pest into a sight to behold. He made a little chuckling sound, began to urinate on his legs and beard, and courted the fair maiden in anything but a subtle manner. She was quite impressed by his antics, and nature took its course. Five months later, I found three babies in the barn, little Amos miniatures. They were perfect.

We learned a lot about life on the little farm. Life and death are lived out in real time, and blessings and curses flow in streams. Animals demand routine and stability. The animal caretaker, in turn, receives those things back. Life takes on a sameness that is comforting, albeit confining. Animals don't care if it is Christmas or Easter or if everyone in the house has the flu. Feeding time is the same, milking time is the same—no excuses, no exceptions.

My cheesemaking adventures continued, and soon I mastered a decent chèvre and other types of fresh cheese. I went on to cheddar and colby, never truly understanding what I was doing and why, but loving every minute of it. I began to barter and trade with neighbors: their produce for my cheese.

What is there about the animals that becomes a part of life? There is a particular intimacy between a dairy cow and dairy farmer. It is the same with goats and sheep. I know of no other relationships that are more trusting and giving. Does everyone who owns "livestock" feel this way? Does a cattle farmer become bonded with his stock, a pork producer with his sows? To some extent, I imagine so. However, knowing the terminal ends of those beasts, self-preservation will not allow those attachments to become too strong. Goats, cows, and sheep charm their way into your heart. Long-term relationships develop with dependencies forming on both accounts. Bossy becomes a member of the family. Amos would liked to have joined us at the dinner table. Even my parents came around to my way of thinking, and I've seen my mother rock a sick baby goat with all the care of a loving grandmother. Though my dad passed away before I was full swing into farming, he knew I was headed in that direction. I believe he watches over me and still shakes his head, saying, "What in the world is she thinking?"

Life has come full circle: I now make cheese again, in the kitchen—small-scale artisan production. I share my love of the art through writing, teaching, and sharing the finished products. My husband, Charlie, and I have two goats

Milk cans await, heavy with their day's product.

and barter for cow's milk. Charlie milks alongside me and is learning to make cheese. My son, now grown, is here visiting, and today he ladled curds into the mold. We look back and laugh about our mistakes, shake our heads over our ignorances and the lessons learned the hard way. We began again.

A lot has changed in the world of agriculture over the past few years. The family farm is coming back, and local food production is in full swing. It is thrilling to see what has happened with the artisan-cheese industry in the United States. What a reward to see small creameries coming back into being. Some may see cheese as food. But after you read this book and see all that goes into each wheel, each block, each piece of this creation, it is my hope you will see it as a work of art.

To all those with a dream, press on. Throughout each day, we are built to search for meaning, asking all the important questions: Why am I here? What is my purpose? What is the true meaning of life? I found the answers to many of these questions while tilling the soil, picking the tomatoes, and of course, milking the goats. Like everyone else, I still have those questions that remain unanswered. Perhaps we are simply not meant to have all the knowledge we seek. Time will tell.

Lately, I have been thinking a lot about a cow. Charlie looks worried. I hear a hen cackle, and I smile, knowing the seed is in full bloom.

Join me on the journey of cheese. Throughout this book you will find profiles of professional cheesemakers, most of whom learned cheesemaking in their own kitchens, just like you will. Recipes and make procedures have been adapted to the home cheesemaker. Photos are included of commercial equipment to illustrate the possibilities, assist you in the understanding of commercial cheesemaking process, and complete the storytelling process.

Without the cooperation, good will, and submissions of those interviewed, this book would not be possible. Every effort has been made to give proper credit for all works cited. Thank you to my friends and colleagues for your contributions. Always remember, "Blessed are the cheesemakers."

CHAPTER 1

Understanding Cheese

Chèvre created by Vermont Butter
and Cheese and served with dried
apricots and roasted walnuts.

Cheesemaking began many centuries ago with a clear case of serendipity. Though no history is formally recorded, legend tells the tale of a nomad carrying milk in a bag made of a calf's stomach. As he traversed rocky desert terrain, the heat of the day

combined with the enzyme released from the carrying pouch to create a chemical reaction. The traveler began his journey with his milk sloshing back and forth in his bag. When he reached his destination, he must have been surprised to see a semisolid substance in the pouch. He probably did not understand the process, but he must have tasted this puzzling creation and thought he had stumbled on to a good thing. As he shared his discovery with others in his community, they too found this new substance to be quite agreeable. Through trial and error, the circumstances that produced this delight were recreated, and cheesemaking became a regular activity within nomadic tribes. Undoubtedly, these early cheesemakers were using goat milk, as in the desert conditions, goats were able to thrive and produce where cows were unable to do so.

The news of this discovery apparently traveled, as cheese became a commonly known food in most regions of the world. If there is a dairy animal present, there will also be cheese. The cheesemaking techniques are similar everywhere, with variations on the central theme of milk, heat, agitation, and enzymes. While some of the procedures for the making of cheese are specific to a variety or a particular place, overall, the process follows a similar pattern. In early times, before reliable refrigeration, cheesemaking was the only way to preserve milk for the inevitable dry spell. Dairy animals, being of seasonal lactation, do have a period of the year when they cease milk production. Aged cheese added a valuable measure of nutrition to what we can only assume was a sparse diet.

When modern-day science entered the picture, an understanding of the chemical process involved in cheesemaking developed. Amazingly, little has changed since the early times. First milk is warmed, and then a bacterial culture is added, followed by rennet, which is still produced from a calf's stomach. The culture acidifies the milk, and the rennet causes the milk to thicken, creating the gel that will become cheese. The rennet and culture continue to work during the aging process, bringing the cheese into maturity.

Recipe Contents

Fresh milk from a Jersey cow, rich with cream. The cheeses include, from left rear, an English cheddar and Swiss, two Camemberts, Capriole Cheese's famous Wabash Cannonball, Cypress Grove's Humboldt Fog (with its ash layer), Cowgirl Creamery's Mt. Tam, and a Muenster.

The manufacture of cheese has become somewhat of a mystery in our modern-day world. Most people have only a vague concept of how cheese is actually made. At one time, education was at hand as small creameries dotted rural landscapes. However, after the Industrial Revolution, cheesemaking became largely known as an automated process, and the small creameries all but disappeared. Time and so-called progress changed the agricultural community entirely. Man and horse power were replaced by mechanics, processing facilities, and automation. While the efficiency of production increased, the art that once belonged to the craftsman became a rare commodity.

Thankfully, times are changing. Local food production has found its audience, and newfound value has been placed on regional, handmade and homegrown food. Cheese is once again returning to local agricultural endeavors. Small creameries are springing up across the United States, and artisan-style products are readily available. Most of these small companies began with one animal or the purchase of milk from a local source, an ordinary kitchen, and a desire to learn about cheesemaking. Presumably, readers of this book have a similar interest, and just as many of the entrepreneurs featured in this book began cheesemaking, so can you! Cheesemakers are part artist and part scientist, taking a liquid substance (milk) and changing it into a solid (cheese). Skill will develop over time, and an instinctual knowledge of what to do next will come.

Milk: The Primary Ingredient

Small-scale cheesemaking is possible today both on a farm or in the middle of the city. Raw milk can often be purchased from local dairy farmers. Make sure the milk is clean and fresh before you make a purchase. Ask to taste it.

continued on page 14

Baetje Farm

When Veronica and Steve Baetje moved to Missouri three years ago, they followed a dream and a vision of their future. Now, sixty Saanen goats later, the couple is immersed in their calling. After years of working with goats and making cheese for family and friends, they achieved their goal of establishing a licensed dairy and cheesemaking plant in 2007. Veronica says, "It is quite a process to go from small-scale goatkeeping and making cheese in one's kitchen to having a processing plant on the farm and selling to the public." For the Baetjes, the end result has been worth all the effort involved.

Best friends throughout their youth, the couple married in their early twenties. "We had a dream to move to the country. At the same time, we were emerging ourselves deeper into our faith. I wanted to experience the things we read about in the Bible: spinning, baking bread, caring for animals, and other things," Veronica says. Their search led them to a conservative Mennonite community, and they soon converted to the Mennonite faith.

Without electricity, Veronica learned to make cheese from her little herd of six goats. Steve, a talented carpenter and stonemason, built "a little goat palace" for Veronica and her milking does. "I would faithfully troop out to milk, twice a day, with my milk pail in one hand, kerosene lantern in the other. I found such peace while out with the goats," Veronica says. The milk quickly started adding up. "I couldn't throw it away. So I started making butter, yogurt, and cheese with five gallons of milk at a time."

Eventually, the couple was able to buy their own farmstead, including a big red barn, 3.7 acres of land, a house, and small pasture. Located an hour east of St. Louis, their small farm combines the best of old and new. Their barn is slightly newer than their home, which was built in the late 1700s.

The big red barn is the centerpiece of Baetje Farm. The original part of the barn was built in the late 1700s. Friends and family came and helped with the addition. "We had an old-time barn raising," remembers Veronica Baetje. It is hard to tell where the old part of the barn stops and the new part begins. The old millstone displays Coeur de la Crème, in Veronica Baetje's favorite heart shape. BAETJE FARM

The Baetjes dress in plain clothing, according to their Mennonite faith, and little would one suspect how much technology they employ in their cheese-making operation. A custom-designed water chiller controls heat and humidity. Monitors track the aging-room conditions. Reminders on Veronica's cell phone assist her in tracking the time for various cheesemaking chores. The cheesemaking room is sparkling and efficient. But despite all the technological help, running the farm and dairy is a demanding job.

"This is the hardest job I have ever had in my life—no vacations, little sleep, and constant work to do. It is not for the fainthearted," Veronica says. "We help birth the kids, bottle feed, milk the does, fix the fence, haul the hay and feed, shovel the manure, wash and sanitize the milking equipment, make the cheese and market the product, plus do all the bookwork and manage the customer accounts. There is little time for anything else besides eating and sleeping. It is beyond a full time job!"

"I wanted to learn what it was like to be a shepherd," says Veronica Baetje. "We couldn't afford a cow when we first started out. So we bought a goat. It was all a part of God's plan," she says. With sixty does to look after, goat care is almost a full time job. BAETJE FARM

Saanen goats take center stage at the Baetje's farm. At milking time, each goat knows the routine and looks forward to the high point of the day. Glancing into the barn, one sees a sea of white goats, lazing in their stalls and looking quite content. As they come and go, stepping out into the pasture, they have the look of satisfaction. It is as if they know their contributions fuel the efforts of the farm. Careful attention to their feed ration, which is all natural, routine care, and lots of love puts sparkle in their eyes. "It really is all about the goats. I am finally a shepherd," Veronica says emphatically.

The area where the Baetjes chose to settle, St. Genevieve, Missouri, was originally settled by French immigrants. The couple's goat-milk, French-style chèvres—Coeur de La Crème (which is molded in a heart-shaped mold and seasoned with organic herbs); Coeur du Clos, a Camembert type; Fleur de la Vallee, a small, washed rind similar to reblochon; Bloomsdale, a Valençay style; and Sainte Genevieve, similar to Chaource—are certainty reminiscent of their imported relatives. The couple currently produces about 300 pounds (136 kg) of cheese a week. They are committed to remaining small and producing artisan-style products.

The Baetjes are largely self-taught cheesemakers. As well as doing their own research, they have attended classes at the University of Wisconsin, and Veronica completed the advanced cheesemaking course at the University of Vermont's Institute of Artisan Cheese program.

As Veronica fills her heart-shaped molds with fresh curds, she concludes, "I am very grateful to be able to be a farmstead cheesemaker. It is truly a dream come true for me. I hope I can still be doing this when I am eighty years old." ♦

continued from page 11

Off-tasting or sour-smelling milk will make off-tasting and sour-smelling cheese, so start off right! Laws governing raw milk sales vary from region to region. Check with the local health department or state department of agriculture to learn about the legality of purchasing raw milk. Pasteurization is important, as the process destroys harmful bacteria capable of causing illness and disease in

Small-scale cheesemakers are making their mark on the local food scene. This wonderful array was produced in Missouri by Veronica Baetje of Baetje Farm. Artisan-scale production allows the cheesemaker to know each piece of cheese. This close attention to detail is displayed from the beginning of the process to the labeling and wrapping at the end. Veronica Baetje's fascination with French-style cheese is evident in this display of the pyramid-shaped Valençay, the heart-shaped Coeur du Clos, a Chaource, and a reblochon (farthest to the left).

humans. If raw milk is purchased, pasteurization is recommended, unless you're making raw-milk cheese, which we will discuss later.

Harmful bacteria in milk has a phenomenal self-replication rate, and bacteria counts increase every hour. It is easy to see how milk that has not been properly refrigerated can quickly become a problem. In his report "Hygiene and Food Safety in Cheesemaking" from the Vermont Institute of Artisan Cheese, Todd Prichard cites these statistics: "Temperature abuse is the #1 cause of food borne illness. Food must be moved through the Danger Zone as rapidly as possible. We must control the growth of unwanted bacteria or they will rapidly increase in numbers and potentially spoil the end product. Bacteria multiply exponentially (i.e., 1>2>4>8). It will only take 20 generations for one bacterium to become 1 million bacterium." Proper cooling and refrigeration of milk is essential. Safety first.

Cream-line milk is available in major grocery stores. The cream has not been separated from this milk, so a thick layer of real cream rests at the top of the bottle. This milk has been pasteurized and will work well for the small-scale cheesemaker. For our purposes, whole milk (milk that has not been separated) will be used.

Home Milk Pasteurization

Pasteurizing milk at home on the stovetop is a simple process. An added bonus is that your milk won't have to stand up to shipping and prolonged storage, so you can pasteurize it safely using lower heat and taking less time than many industrial milk producers use, thus retaining the necessary bacteria for cheesemaking. All you need is a double boiler or two stainless-steel pots and a kitchen thermometer. Then just follow these simple steps:

1. Pour the milk into the smaller of the two pots, and place the small pot inside the larger pot, with three inches (7.6 cm) of water in the bottom.

2. Slowly heat the milk to 145°F (63°C) and hold the temperature there for thirty minutes. Stir the milk gently throughout the process to make sure it is evenly heated.

3. Remove the milk from heat and place it in a sink filled with ice, to bring the temperature down as quickly as possible. When the milk reaches 40°F (4°C), it is chilled and may be stored in the refrigerator until ready for use.

To further explain the chemical processes of cheesemaking is to understand the composition of milk. Basically, milk is composed of water, lactose, fat, protein, minerals, and miscellaneous components, such as enzymes, vitamins, somatic cells. The goal in cheesemaking is to isolate the solids in the milk, then to expel most of the moisture. The liquid removed during this process is whey. Whey is considered a waste product, except in the manufacture of ricotta or other whey-based cheese. It is also used within the health industry as a nutritional supplement. To make cheese, the cheesemaker brings milk to the temperature required to promote the growth of the bacteria that feed on lactose.

Do not purchase UHT milk for making cheese. UHT stands for *ultra heat treated*. Due to the high temperatures involved in the manufacture of a shelf-stable

The Three Commandments of Sanitation

For the purposes of this book, I will assume these three things regarding sanitation:

1. The reader will supply a clean working environment. Hands and nails will be scrubbed thoroughly before any cheesemaking begins.

2. All equipment will be sanitized; this means pots, molds (for shaping cheese), spoons, ladles, cloths, knives, mats, and so on.

3. Milk purchased for cheesemaking will be from a reliable source and pasteurized according to directions. Raw milk products must be aged sixty days or more to be considered a safe food.

product, *all* bacteria contained in the milk is destroyed. Milk normally contains bacterial flora that can be enhanced by the addition of manmade cultures. However, when milk is exposed to the extremely high temperatures required for UHT, it is no longer suitable for cheesemaking. No bacteria, no cheese.

Sanitation

Cleanliness of utensils, work surfaces, and cooking pots is of utmost importance in cheesemaking. Bacterial contamination will occur if strict sanitation procedures are not developed and followed.

To sanitize equipment, fill your clean kitchen sink with tap water; add one cap of regular household chlorine bleach to sanitize utensils, pots, and cheese molds. Or take a tip from homebrewers of beer and wine, and use One-Step Sanitizer, an easy cleaner that requires no bleach or rinsing. Sanitize your equipment before you begin making cheese, and allow the equipment to air dry. Wash any cloth towels or cheesecloth in a mild bleach solution before and after use.

Cheesemaking Techniques

Over time you will develop specific cheesemaking techniques.

Words not spoken or performed in the cheese room include *beat*, *whip*, *mash*, and *chop*. Cheesemaking is a gentle art, especially on the home-kitchen scale. Think Zen. Milk is fragile. If it is handled roughly, the fat cells, which are needed for the creation of cheese, will break down. So gentle handling of the milk is crucial to the cheesemaking process.

Here are some general tips to guide the new cheesemaker to success:

• Use one gallon of milk as a base line. In the beginning, do not increase the amount, just in case things do not go as planned. Pasteurize the milk, as explained.

• Set aside some uninterrupted time for the first venture into cheesemaking. Have all equipment ready and milk on hand. Cheesemaking requires patience, and attempts at shortcuts will lead to failures.

Happy goats at Vermont Butter and Cheese.

• Cultures are delicate beings. Always use a clean and dry spoon to retrieve the culture from its foil pouch. Add the specified amount to the warmed milk. Immediately close the pouch, clip it closed with a paper clip, and then place the foil pouch in a zip-top plastic bag. Refrigerate.

• If the make procedure calls for more than one culture, be careful not to cross contaminate one culture with another. Use a separate clean and dry measuring spoon for each type of culture.

continued on page 20

Redwood Hill Farm and Creamery

Jennifer Bice is one of the fortunate few who have found their true calling in life. After thirty-one years of goat dairying, Bice still maintains her enthusiasm for her goats, her cheese and yogurt, and her way of life. A dairy herd numbering more than 300 head, the goats are hard-working members of the Redwood Hill team.

Bice began her life's work when she was ten years old, when her family moved from Los Angeles to Sonoma County, California. "There were no sidewalks for skating and bike riding and no other neighbor kids to play with," Bice relates. Her parents thought the activities of a small farm might fill in the empty spots and ease the transition to their new location.

"We had different animals, and the goats quickly became our favorites. They were more like dogs in their personalities, and they learned to do tricks. We each wanted to have our own goats, and so it added up to a herd quite quickly. So my parents built a dairy, and we all milked before school. My dad bottled milk, and my mom and I delivered it. Of course, this period of time was the beginning of the natural foods movement, so raw goat milk was in high demand," Bice says.

The family first began producing goat milk in glass bottles in a grade-A dairy in 1968 and later branched into kefir and cheese. In 1978, Bice and her late husband took over the dairy and began to make yogurt in addition to cheese.

"I learned to make cheese by reading books [and] trial and error," Bice remembers. "I took a short course at Cal Poly Tech [California Polytechnic State University] to gain a working knowledge of cheesemaking. Eventually I was able to go to France and learn more."

Jennifer Bice pictured with Redwood Hill Farm goat, Jambalaya, a grand champion at the Sonoma County Fair. Jambalaya is a past national grand champion Alpine and one of the most highly awarded dairy goats in the country. Bice's love of the goats has always come first. Redwood Hill goats are highly regarded within the dairy goat industry. REDWOOD HILL

Bice's focus on the goats brought her to a place of respect and high esteem within the dairy-goat industry. Her farm, Redwood Hill, is well known for its genetics program and the excellence of her milking herd. The herd is shown on a national level and consistently receives awards, including national championships in four of the breeds recognized by the American Dairy Goat Association. Her breeding stock is in demand, and she provides animals to goat breeders across North America and South America. She has served as a dairy-goat judge for the past thirty-one years and judged the prestigious American Dairy Goat Association National Show six times.

As the first "Certified Humane" goat dairy in the United States, Redwood Hill sets a fine example for other dairy farms to follow. The Certified Humane precise standards, set forth by the Humane Farm Animal Care organization, ensure the animals are well cared for. The goats at Redwood Hill are all registered with the American Dairy Goat Association. Goats selected to be a member of this elite group are chosen because of their milk's flavor and their body conformation, as well as other attributes.

Bice is also a frequent speaker, presenting in various forums, including Slow Food USA. She subscribes to sustainable-agricultural practices and partners-in-conservation techniques through the Sonoma Land Trust and Co-op America.

Her advice to those who might be thinking of a dairy or cheesemaking as a vocation: "I suggest anyone interested work first in an operation similar to what they would want to start, to see all that is involved. I have seen so many people over the years that get started, but then can't really do it. They go out due to the amount of work and labor intensiveness of it all."

The Redwood Hill product range is broad and includes California crottin, which has been awarded Best in Show at the American Dairy Goat Association National Cheese Competition, twice voted Best Farmstead Goat Cheese at the American Cheese Society, and chosen as the best crottin—better than the French originals—in a recent *Wall Street Journal* tasting. Gravenstein Gold, the farm's newest cheese, is a raw-milk cheese with a rind washed in local cider. Feta, cheddar, smoked cheddar, and Chèvre Camellia (a bloomy rind) complete the list. Redwood Hill Farm's European-style yogurt is also highly decorated and has won numerous gold medals.

"I think artisan cheese will continue to become more popular in the United States," Bice says. "People are much more aware of the food they eat today. . . . It is more than the taste today; it is voting for what your support by where you spend your food dollars." ◆

Redwood Hill Farm's goats are mixed breeds. Pictured are the pure white Saanens, the black and white Toggenburg, the pure black a Nubian cross (note the airplane ears, typical of a Nubian cross), and an Oberhausli.
REDWOOD HILL

Jennifer Bice at work in the creamery, creating a block of feta. The feta will be aged in a salt brine. Goat milk adds a complexity to feta, as does the addition of lipase. Feta can also be made with sheep or cow milk.
REDWOOD HILL

continued from page 17

• When heating milk for cheesemaking, do so with a low flame, being careful to avoid scorching.

• A timer is a cheesemaker's best friend. After you achieve a comfort level with the process, you will have other tasks to tend to instead of watching the pot. When that happens, set the timer. Time does fly, and it is easy to forget about the pot on the stove. The timer is a most valuable tool in the cheese kitchen.

• A good thermometer is one of the most helpful tools you can have. Temperature is one of the key components to good cheesemaking, so a thermometer is an invaluable and necessary addition to the basic equipment required for cheesemaking.

• Cheesecloth has come a long way. There is a synthetic blend perfect for draining curds. Traditional cheesecloth is often too thin to capture the curd, so the synthetic or a more traditional cloth, butter muslin, makes the best choice for draining. Nylon parachute fabric, usually available at fabric stores, also works wonderfully. It has the qualities of being porous enough to allow the whey to drain, yet captures even tiny bits of curd. Cheese-supply houses also offer draining bags, which provide an easy way to drain curds and whey.

How to Make a Draining Bag

Purchase nylon parachute fabric from your local source. One yard will make two medium size bags.

Begin by cutting the yard of fabric in half. The fabric is 45 inches (114.3 cm) wide, so you will have two 18- by 45-inch (45.7- by 114.3-cm) pieces of fabric. First turn down the top edge ½ inch (13 mm), then press with a hot iron. Turn down the top edge again, this time 1 inch (25.5 mm), press, and stitch all the way around.

Now fold the fabric in half to form what will be more or less a pillowcase. Seam around all three edges, and then go back and serge or zigzag the seam—something to keep the edges of the fabric from fraying. You don't want strings in your cheese!

After you are finished sewing, turn the bag so the stitching is to the inside of the bag. Wash your new bag, and it is ready to use.

After it is filled with curd, use a length of nylon cord to gather the top of the bag together, and then hang the bag over the kitchen sink or other area where it will be free to drain.

If you don't sew, draining bags are available for purchase. When washing a draining bag after use, turn it inside out and remove all bits of leftover cheese. Then wash it in hot water. Add a capful of bleach as a sanitizing agent.

Recordkeeping

Recordkeeping is essential to cheesemaking. Perhaps your first time out you create the best cheese of all time. Then what? Of course, you would like to recreate that exact same cheese. But the chances of doing that are quite slim if you did not keep records or if your recorded events and times are not accurate. One of the primary components required in successful cheesemaking is a repeatable process. The key to this process is recordkeeping.

A make sheet is the place to keep your records. This sheet will help you either avoid repeating a disaster where something went terribly wrong or provide a valuable tool for recreating a masterpiece. Expect to have both experiences.

There are some days when cheesemaking is an uphill battle. For those experienced with making yeast breads, the challenges may be familiar. There are those days when the bread won't rise, days when the dough seems tough, or days when other critical steps simply don't happen. Once in a while, such days will happen in the cheesemaking. The culture may not be fresh, the rennet could be old, and milk is an ever-changing palette. There are many variables, and once in a while there may be a batch that simply doesn't go as planned. Don't lament over it. Remember the old adage, don't cry over spilled milk. This applies to cheese as well. Try and try again.

Here is a typical make sheet. Create your own version of it.

Cheese Make Sheet

Date: _____

Type of Cheese: _____

Milk

Type of Milk: _____

Quantity of Milk: _____

Milk Initially Heated to What Temperature: _____

Culture

Type of Culture: _____

Quantity of Culture: _____

Time Culture Added: _____

Rennet

Type of Rennet: _____

Quantity of Rennet: _____

Time Rennet Added: _____

Curd

Time Until Curd Set: _____

Time Curd Was Cut: _____

Size of Curd: _____

Was the Curd Cooked? _____

Was the Curd Washed? _____

Mold

Type of Molds: _____

Quantity of Molds: _____

Pressing

Was Cheese Pressed? _____

How Cheese Was Pressed: _____

Weight of Press: _____

Length of Pressing: _____

Salting

Quantity of Salt: _____

How Salt Was Added (brine, direct, added to curd, etc.): _____

Aging

Aging Time: _____

Aging Temperature: _____

Flavor Notes:

_____
_____
_____
_____

Goatsbeard Farm

This sign marks the entrance to Goatsbeard Farm. A lush, peaceful valley in central Missouri provides the perfect farm setting for the small farm. Ken and Jenn Muno, their sons, and fifty milking goats call it home. The Munos have been making cheese for the past seven years, using traditional cheesemaking techniques combined with their own avant-garde methods.

When asked how she and her husband, Ken, got into the cheesemaking business, Jenn Muno says, "We both loved goat cheese. We knew we wanted to make cheese, but neither of us were raised on a farm or had any knowledge of animal husbandry. We thought goats would be more manageable than cows. They are so smart and enjoyable to be around. When working as closely as we do with the animals, that is an important factor!"

"We began with five goats. . . . We are now up to fifty-seven," Ken adds. "I apprenticed with a farm in California and learned a lot about cheesemaking there. I fell in love with farming and wanted to do something related to food. We didn't consider any other animals. The goats have been the focus all along."

The Munos' farm, Goatsbeard Farm in central Missouri, is known for a variety of cheese types and styles. Its fresh chèvre captured first place in the American Dairy Goat Association Cheese Competition in 2005. This cheese is made utilizing traditional French-style methods, in which the cheese is molded in small, perforated cups that allow the whey to drain away from the curd. Additions such as herbes de Provence, black pepper, or garlic make this chèvre a versatile product. The farm's other types of cheese include a spreadable blend, available with added herbs, garlic, or chipotle, packed in tubs; a marinated cheese packed in olive oil; and a Greek-style feta.

The Munos also make aged blends, some of which are quite complicated. Prairie Bloom, for example, is a white-mold-ripened variety with a light mushroomy taste, similar in style to a French Brie. This cheese takes time, proper aging conditions, and patience to create. Other aged products include three raw-milk varieties: Osage Orange, a washed-rind Muenster done in a European style; Walloon, an aged hard cheese that has a nutty flavor and is suitable for slicing and grating; and Moniteau Blue, a rich, piquant blue cheese that is delicious crumbled over a salad or served with fruit. These cheeses are aged sixty days or more. A small aging room keeps the cheeses at the appropriate temperature and humidity to bring them to successful maturity. The Munos offer serving suggestions and recipes to complement their cheeses.

The goats at Goatsbeard Farm are carefully maintained and fed daily rations to keep them at top production. A healthy goat is a good producer, so proper care is crucial to the continued success of the dairy. The goats are obviously well cared for and

happy in their environment. Ken rotates them through a maze of paddocks, providing them with a fresh supply of grass and hay. Twice a day, each morning and evening, the goats arrive at the barnyard gate at the appointed time in anticipation of milking and dinner.

Four part-time employees and one newly appointed intern, assist in the daily chores, beginning with milking, cleaning before and after milking, and caring for the animals.

Then there are cheeses to set, molds to wash, and products to package.

Ken and Jenn not only consider the environmental impact of their operation, but also the bottom line. As with any small business, keeping costs at bay is key to longevity. Ken has myriad innovative and cost-saving ideas in place. Their home, the dairy, and the plant are all heated with wood. Everything from the cheesemaking vat to the hot water for wash down begins at the outdoor wood furnace. Ken says, "It feels really good to do this work with the heat supplied by wood. The wood, in essence, has become a part of the cheese. I am proud of that."

All Goatsbeard products currently sell as quickly as they become available. The Munos emphasize quality over quantity, and when asked about expansion, Ken says they are about as big as they care to be. Their direct connection with their customers, through farmers' markets, has made them quite popular and made the Munos local celebrities. ◆

Ladies in waiting. These crossbred goats are heavy producers. The average daily yield of a goat is a little less than one gallon per day.

Ken Muno at work in the cheese room. With a thermometer in hand, he checks the temperature of the curd in the vat. Today's make is chèvre, one of Goatsbeard Farm's most popular products.

Cheesemaking Step by Step

These images illustrate the creation of a molded goat cheese, using basket style molds. Crottin or pyramid molds may be used in place of the baskets.

1. Pour the milk gently into your large cooking pot, and heat the milk slowly to 86°F (30°C) over medium heat.

2. Add the culture, and stir in the culture thoroughly using a top to bottom motion. Let sit for the time specified in the recipe.

3. Add the rennet. Some recipes will require you add the rennet drop by drop; others have you dilute the rennet in water and add the solution.

4. After adding the rennet to the milk, stir, top to bottom, for one minute.

5. Cover and allow the renneted milk to rest, undisturbed, for thirty minutes

6. After slicing through the curd, go back with the knife and pick up the curd to see if there is a clean separation.

7. The curd after cutting. Note the curds are all about the same size. Let the curds rest for 15 minutes after the cut is complete. This resting period allows the curds time to heal and toughen up.

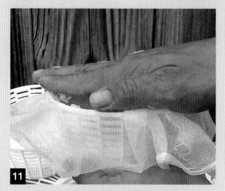

8. While the cut curds are resting, prepare the cheese baskets by lining them with disposable cheesecloth. Place the baskets on a rack above a bowl or bucket that will catch the whey.

9. Gently ladle the curd into the lined baskets. The curds will compress as the whey is expelled, so expect the cheese to be about half the size of the original mold.

10. Fill the baskets to the top. Let the curds settle for two hours and then top off again. Allow the curds to drain for twelve hours. These curds will shrink to about half their original size.

11. For a more even appearance, after six hours remove the cheese from the mold and flip it, the top becoming the bottom. Put the cheese back in the mold.

12. After twelve hours of draining, carefully take the cheese from the basket and place on the drying rack.

13. Salt the cheese to taste.

Chèvre

We will begin with a simple, fresh cheese, chèvre, which is one of the most basic of cheeses and a classic from France. Chèvre is only made from goat milk, so make an acquaintance with your local goat farmer. Chèvre is French for "goat." According to my French auntie, Elaine, the proper pronunciation is "chev."

This cheese is commonly produced in France by farmstead cheesemakers. It can be made with a minimum of skill, ingredients, and equipment, which makes it a perfect project for the beginning cheesemaker. A few purchases will be required to begin cheesemaking, so plan ahead to have the necessary equipment on hand.

EQUIPMENT	INGREDIENTS
Slotted spoon	1 gallon pasteurized goat milk
Ladle	⅛ teaspoon Mesophilic DVI MA culture
String	2 drops of liquid rennet dissolved in ¼ cup
Colander	nonchlorinated water
	½ to 1 teaspoon noniodized salt to taste
	Optional: Herbs, such as fresh chives, lavender blossoms, or a blend, such as herbes de Provence; other ingredients, such as black pepper, green peppers, or olives

Chèvre Uses and Pairings

Chèvre is one of the most famous—and favorite—goat cheeses in the world. Known for its distinctive tang or bite, this cheese is quite versatile.

Chèvre is the perfect topping for French bread. That crusty loaf, sliced and paired with the cheese is a simple, yet elegant combination. Add fresh grapes, a glass of rosé—what more could one ask for?

"A loaf of bread, a jug of wine, and thou," as ancient Persian poet Omar Khayyám wrote. What about the cheese? Add chèvre, and this scenario is indeed perfect.

Chèvre pairs well with vegetables. Split snow peas and stuff them with chèvre; score cherry tomatoes and fill them with chevre for a summer treat. Chèvre is frequently used in salads and even for dessert. The French feature cheese plates on their dessert menu and offer a wide array, including chèvre.

The classic blend of herbes de Provence will enhance this cheese, as will lavender. Lavender flowers can be added to chèvre in small amounts, and the flavor will bring a subtle floral bouquet to the cheese. The color of the flowers adds an unexpected visual element. Serve this lavender chèvre for dessert and serve it drizzled in honey, paired with a ladyfinger cookie or a gingersnap.

Pour the goat milk into a cooking pot. Heat milk slowly to 86°F (30°C). Remove from heat.

Sprinkle the culture over the top of the milk and gently stir, making sure the culture is dissolved and well integrated into the milk. Allow this mixture to sit for about 45 minutes, so the culture has time to develop.

Add the rennet mixed in water and stir, coming up from the bottom of the pot, until the culture and rennet are well integrated into the milk. Let the mixture rest, covered with a cloth, in a warm place for 12 to 18 hours. The gel will thicken to the consistency of yogurt while it is resting.

When the gel has thickened, it is time to ladle the mass into a draining bag. Line a colander with the draining bag, cheesecloth, or muslin. Place the colander in the sink. With a slotted spoon, gently transfer the gel mass, now called the **curd**, into the lined colander. Keep ladling until all the curd is in the colander. The leftover liquid is the **whey**, which is a waste product. Once all the curd is in the colander, gather the draining bag and tie it with the string. Hang it over the sink, and the whey will drain, rapidly at first, then more slowly.

Chèvre encrusted with herbes de Provence.

Herbes de Provence

This classic Provençal blend of herbs seems to show up in almost everything I cook! It's great on chicken, on salmon, or on top of freshly baked breads, and it is the perfect complement to chèvre.

The combination of herbs is quite forgiving, so adjust the amount to your taste. Try herbes de Provence as a ready made product or make your own blend if you have access to fresh herbs.

INGREDIENTS

3 tablespoons savory
3 tablespoons thyme
2 tablespoons marjoram
1 teaspoon basil
1 teaspoon lavender
½ teaspoon sage
½ teaspoon fennel

A note about lavender: lavender is quite underrated and underused in the culinary arts. I love the thought—and taste—of adding the floral bouquet lavender offers to various foods. This herb perfectly complements sweets and looks lovely when blended with icings on cakes or cookies. Try a fresh chèvre made with a little lavender placed in the mold while the curd is drained. I have friends who request this cheese frequently.

Crème Fraiche

Crème fraiche has been elevated to celebrity status due to the popularity of television cooking shows. This French cheese is a light accent and used to top fruit cobblers, berries, and other sweets. Many recipes require the addition of crème fraiche, and it is often served as a side garnish or topping. Its consistency is similar to that of sour cream, and it has a slightly sweet, sometimes nutty flavor.

Crème fraiche is made in the same way as quark or chèvre; simply omit the rennet. The texture will be soft and creamy; the tangy flavor is the perfect complement to fresh fruits. Imagine strawberry short-cake with crème fraiche between the layers.

Crème fraiche also accents dishes with a savory element. Try it on top of pumpkin soup or borscht.

Crème fraiche laced with strawberries and peaches.

Two things are happening while the curd drains: Acid is developing, so the flavor of the cheese is coming to life. And the moisture ratio of liquid to solid is dropping; therefore, the consistency and the stability of the finished product are changing. Chèvre is meant to be soft, so the moisture level will remain high. But this high moisture makes chèvre less stable than other aged or hard cheeses, so it should be consumed within a few days of **the make**. (In the language of cheese, the process of creating the cheese is called "the make.")

Allow the curd to drain for about 12 hours. Then remove the curd from the bag, place it in a bowl, and work in the salt. Salting has a number of purposes in the cheesemaking process. It adds flavor, promotes the shedding of moisture, and retards bacteria growth. Salt can be added directly to the curd, used to develop the rind on the cheese with a direct rub, or added to water to create brine, which the cheese can be placed in.

Flavor with herbs or other ingredients. These ingredients can be added to the cheese to make a spread, or the cheese can be rolled into logs or rounds and then rolled in the herbs. Chèvre is somewhat bland, so it will take on the flavors of the condiments or herbs added to it.

To store, place in a covered dish. Best served at room temperature.

Quark

Quark is the cow-milk equivalent of chèvre and is widely used in European cuisine as a baking cheese. Few cheesemakers manufacture this cheese in the United States, so make your own!

INGREDIENTS
1 gallon pasteurized cow milk
⅛ teaspoon Mesophilic DVI MA culture
2 drops of liquid rennet dissolved in ¼ cup nonchlorinated water
noniodized salt

Following the same instructions as for chèvre, simply substitute whole cow milk for the goat milk.

Pour the cow milk into a cooking pot. Heat milk slowly to 86°F (30°C). Remove from heat.

Sprinkle the culture over the top of the milk; gently stir, making sure the culture is dissolved and well integrated into the milk. Allow this mixture to sit for about 45 minutes, so the culture has time to develop.

Add the rennet mixed in water and stir, coming up from the bottom of the pot, until the culture and rennet are well integrated into the milk. Let rest, covered with a cloth, in a warm place for 12 to 18 hours. The gel will thicken to the consistency of yogurt while it is resting.

When the gel has thickened, line a colander with the draining bag, cheesecloth, or muslin. Place the colander in the sink. With a slotted spoon, gently transfer the curd into the lined colander. Keep ladling until all the curd is in the colander. Once it is, gather the draining bag and tie with the string. Hang it over the sink, and the whey will drain, rapidly at first, then more slowly.

Allow the curd to drain for about 12 hours. Then remove the curd from the bag, place it in a bowl, and work in the salt.

To store, place in a covered dish. Best served at room temperature.

Quark Uses and Pairings

- - - - - - - - - - - - -

Quark is *the* cheese for making cheesecakes. It will make the finest cheesecake you've ever experienced. Do not add salt if you are planning to use quark in cheesecake.

Quark is also a marvelous accompaniment to bread or crackers and can be flavored with herbs. You can also enjoy this cheese as a breakfast spread.

Crottin

This classic French goat cheese takes its name from the disc shape of the mold it is formed in, known in France as the *crottin*.

The consistency of crottin is more solid than chèvre, and crottin has a lower moisture content, so it will keep longer. It is not a spread, but a soft cheese.

SPECIAL EQUIPMENT

Crottin molds: These will mold the cheese in the traditional French form, the *crottin*. Use the 3x2¼x⅜-inch (72x57x203 mm) size. Buy at least four molds—and six is better. A pyramid mold is another interesting shape and is a typical shape for goat cheese.

INGREDIENTS

1 gallon pasteurized goat milk
¼ teaspoon Mesophilic DVI MA culture
¼ teaspoon liquid rennet diluted in ¼ cup cool, nonchlorinated water
Noniodized salt
herbs (optional)

Pour the milk into a cooking pot. Heat milk slowly to 86°F (30°C). Remove from heat.

Crottin Uses and Pairings

– – – – –

Slice the crottin and use it on a sandwich. Crumble it for salads or to put on a pizza. It does not melt the same as an Italian cheese; it will simply be soft, not fluid. However, the acidic bite associated with goat milk is a wonderful accent to a rustic pizza.

Fried Goat Cheese

I was first introduced to fried goat cheese by a friend from Palestine. You can make it from scratch, and it's a great way to use up goat cheese that has gone a bit dry. Do not expect goat cheese to melt. It will become soft. Add coarse salt and black pepper to enhance the flavor of the goat milk.

Prepare crottin as directed, but leave the cheese out an extra day until it is quite dry. Slice it in slabs about ½ inch (13 mm) thick. Using a small skillet, heat 3 tablespoons of olive oil. Then add the slabs of cheese. Quickly fry, turning once. Be careful, as the oil will splatter. Remove from heat, and place the melted cheese on fresh bread, crackers, or steak. Add a bit of salt and freshly ground black pepper—and enjoy!

Sprinkle the culture over the top of the milk and gently stir, making sure the culture is dissolved and well integrated into the milk.

Add the rennet mixed in water and stir, coming up from the bottom of the pot, until the culture and rennet are well integrated into the milk. Allow this mixture to sit about 45 minutes, so the culture has time to develop. During this time the milk will coagulate.

After about 20 minutes, test the curd for signs of coagulation. To do this test, simply slice through the curd with a long knife and look for a distinct separation. This separation is a **clean break**. If the curd is not well defined at this point, and there is not a distinct slit in the gel when it is tested, wait 5 more minutes and slice through the mass again. If it looks like yogurt, it is not ready. Test again 5 minutes later. The break should be achieved at 25 to 35 minutes. Achieving the clean break and cutting the curd at the proper time is one of the critical points in cheesemaking. Cut too soon, and the curd will not be well defined, and the result will be too liquid. Cut too late, and the result will be tough curds that do not want to mold properly and will resist all efforts to make good cheese.

Once the clean-break stage is achieved, it is time to cut the curd. For the home cheesemaker, a long knife will work for cutting. Cut the curd in a series of quick movements, traveling from one side of the pot to the other. Next cut in the other direction. This cutting pattern will produce small cubes. Cut quickly. The cubes should be about ½ inch (13 mm) when the cutting is finished. Do not go smaller, or the curds will be too small and will be reduced to mush.

After the cutting is finished, allow the cubed curds to rest for about 10 minutes. This allows them to **heal**.

To fill the molds, be gentle and scoop the curd, trying not to break them into smaller pieces. Fill the molds to the top. Whey will immediately begin to flow from the holes in the molds; set the molds on a rack to drain. Soon the cheese will begin to shrink. Top off the mold once with more curd, simply letting the whey drain from the curd. Allow the molds to sit for about 12 hours at room temperature, approximately 70°F (21°C). If the cheese is made in the evening, the next morning, it will be ready to unmold.

To remove the cheese from the molds, use a table knife, running it between the edge of the cheese and the mold. Quickly turn the mold upside down and rap it on a hard surface. The cheese will dislodge. Allow the crottin to dry for another 4 hours at room temperature.

Now it is time to salt the cheese. Salting is an acquired skill. It is easy to apply too much or too little. Err on the cautious side, and the salt can be increased. Start with ¼ teaspoon per crottin. Place the salt on wax paper, pinch up a bit, and apply to the crottin. Taste and then adjust.

If you would like to add herbs or seasonings, roll each crottin in the desired herb while the cheese is still moist. Recommended herbs include freshly snipped chives, herbes de Provence, coarsely ground black pepper, fresh mint or lemon balm, or fresh lemon thyme. Some cheesemakers add ingredients to their cheese while it is in the curd stage, before it is placed into the mold.

Place the cheese on a drying rack (or a food dehydrator tray works quite well) at room temperature. The cheese should be dry in 4 to 6 hours. It will have developed a bit of a crust, which is fine. Wrap in specialty cheese paper or wax paper. Refrigerate. Due to the high moisture content, it will keep only 15 days. The cheese will be at the peak of flavor when served at room temperature.

Tomato and Goat-Cheese Fondue Recipe

SOURCE: Redwood Hill Farm and Creamery and Chef John Ash

I've always loved fondues, but they can be a little rich. Here's a version that cuts down on the fat, but still provides all of the flavor. Serve this fondue with good crusty, peasant-style bread, which you can use to dip into and scoop up the cheesy mixture.

INGREDIENTS

2 tablespoons olive oil
¼ cup finely chopped shallots or green onions
2 tablespoons finely chopped garlic
3 cups (one 28-ounce can) crushed tomatoes with
    basil (Muir Glen Organic brand preferred)
1 cup hearty red wine
1 tablespoon finely grated orange zest
1 tablespoon each finely chopped parsley and basil
salt and freshly ground black pepper
8 to 10 ounces Redwood Hill Farm's Goat Milk
    Sharp Cheddar

In a large skillet, heat the olive oil over moderate heat, and stir in the shallots and garlic. Sauté until soft but not brown. Add the tomatoes and wine, and simmer uncovered for 5 to 10 minutes until the mixture reduces to a light sauce consistency. Stir in zest and herbs, and season with salt and pepper. Pour the mixture into an attractive six-cup, ovenproof baking dish. Place cheese in the middle of the oven and bake in a preheated 325°F (163.7°C) oven for 15 to 20 minutes or until the cheese is melted. Serve immediately.

Kochkasse

Hermann, Missouri, is in the heart of Missouri wine country. At one time, Hermann was the largest wine-producing region in the United States. Here, long-time residents still make their own wine, beer, sausage, and cheese. Local resident Helen Epple is still going strong and milking her goats each day. She and her husband, Vernon, are an inspiration, keeping a garden, chickens, and supplying for many of their own needs. I might add they are well into their eighties. Helen makes kochkasse.

Kochkasse is a classic German cheese, and the name translates to "cooked cheese." I live in a German settlement, and countless neighbors have told me stories about their grandmothers making this cheese.

INGREDIENTS

2 cups freshly made quark or chèvre
½ cup cow or goat milk
¼ cup butter
½ teaspoon baking soda
salt

Place the quark or chèvre in a large, heavy skillet, and add the milk, butter, baking soda, and a heavy sprinkling of salt. Place the skillet over low heat and stir constantly until the milk and butter are worked in. Cook about 20 minutes, stirring continuously. Continue to cook and stir, over low heat, until the mixture thickens and does not look shiny. The result will be a thick, spreadable cheese. Add black pepper or caraway seeds, if desired.

Store in the refrigerator in a covered container. This spread will keep for about two weeks.

Kochkasse Uses and Pairings

Kochkasse is a staple in the German kitchen, so I guess it should be no surprise that kochkasse pairs well with beer; a lager is the perfect complement. This cheese is often served on crackers or with heavy, dark bread, which is enhanced by cheese's caraway seeds.

Yogurt

SOURCE: Jennifer Bice of Redwood Hill Farm and Creamery

Yogurt made from goat milk is tangy and pleasantly acidic. Often those who are allergic to cow milk can tolerate goat-milk products.

INGREDIENTS

1 gallon fresh, unpasteurized goat or cow milk
1 tablespoon plain yogurt with active cultures or 1 packet freeze-dried culture
    containing lactobacillus

Heat the milk to 108°F (42.2°C). Add the plain yogurt or freeze-dried cultures. Make sure to use yogurt from a new cup and a clean spoon to add the yogurt.

Incubate the milk mixture at 104 to 108°F (40 to 42.2°C). To do this, you can use a home yogurt maker or an incubation device of your own. Some people use a heating pad wrapped around a jar; they put the jar in the oven on low, or place the jar in a crockpot. Whatever you use, experiment with water and a thermometer before you actually make the yogurt, to be sure you can hold the milk at the required temperature. Incubate the milk for 6 to 8 hours, depending on your taste.

When finished incubating, chill the yogurt before eating it, being careful not to agitate or move the yogurt much until it is well chilled.

Goat-milk yogurt will not get as thick as cow-milk yogurt. Many commercial cow-milk yogurts add powdered milk as a thickener. You can also use a small amount of tapioca, which is a natural thickener from the cassava root.

To serve lebneh
as they do in the
Middle East, first
put the cheese on
a plate and form
it into a desired
shape, with a slight
depression in the
middle. Fill the
depression with
olive oil and top
with chopped mint
leaves. Eat the
cheese with toasted
pita-bread slices
or the traditional
cucumber-and-
tomato salad served
at virtually every
meal in Israel.

Many people
prefer to top their
lebneh with zatar,
which is a blend of
herbs, including
oregano, mint,
thyme, and savory.
Zatar is often mixed
with sesame seeds,
salt, and olive oil.

Lebneh

SOURCE: Jennifer Bice of Redwood Hill Farm and Creamery

Lebneh yogurt cheese is widely used in the Middle East and Greece—a fact that results in several spellings of its name, including *lebanah* and *labanah*.

This cheese is the same consistency of cream cheese. It is also easy to make. Simply allow the liquid to drain from the solids. Yogurt funnels are available for this very purpose.

To make yogurt cheese, place 2 cups of plain goat- or cow-milk yogurt in a colander lined with three layers of moistened cheesecloth. Bring the corners of the cheesecloth together to form a bag, which can then be drained over the sink. Let the yogurt drain for 8 to 16 hours. Stir occasionally, scraping the cheese away from the cheesecloth to allow better draining. The longer the yogurt drains the thicker and more tart the yogurt cheese will be.

Kefir

Kefir is a fermented type of milk with a consistency similar to grocery-store yogurt drinks. It's a common drink throughout the Middle East.

INGREDIENTS
1 tablespoon kefir grains
1 quart whole or 2 percent milk

Put kefir grains in a glass jar and fill the jar almost full with the whole milk. Cover with a clean cloth and set aside on your kitchen counter. Wait 1 to 2 days, stirring periodically with a plastic spoon. (Using plastic is particularly important, since metal appears to damage the cultures.) When the milk is thick, strain out the kefir with a plastic strainer (being careful to keep the grains intact). The milk that was strained is ready for use. Rinse the used grains, refill the jar with fresh milk and restart the process.

Next time you wish to make kefir, you can use these same grains, as they will continue to remain active. Just pour them into a glass jar, cover them with water, seal the jar, and refrigerate it.

Amish Cup Cheese

SOURCE: Adapted from Frank Kosikowski's recipe in his 1966 self-published book, *Cheese and Fermented Milk Foods*

The Amish, well-known for their frugality and creative culinary skills, often sold this cheese in a cup, which is how it received its name. A fragrant German cheese, it is often served as a side dish at one of Amish's hearty breakfasts.

INGREDIENTS

1 gallon pasteurized whole milk
¼ teaspoon Mesophilic DVI MA culture
½ teaspoon Penicillum candidum
¼ teaspoon liquid rennet diluted in ¼ cup nonchlorinated water
½ teaspoon baking soda

Place the milk in a large pot and warm it to 90°F (32.2°C). Sprinkle the cultures over the milk and stir them in, stirring top to bottom. Add the rennet in water. Stir.

Let the mixture sit for 30 minutes, or until a clean break is achieved. (See the crottin recipe, earlier in this chapter, for more about achieving a clean break.) Cut the curds into ½-inch (13-mm) cubes and let them rest for 30 minutes.

Cook the curds over low heat. Slowly increase temperature until it reaches 110°F (43.3°C) and hold there for 30 minutes. Stir frequently. Hold the curds at that temperature until they are well formed and spring back to the touch, usually 30 to 40 minutes total.

Line a colander with cheesecloth and ladle the curds into the colander. Drain for 15 minutes. Prepare a bowl of cool water and dip the curds, still contained in the bag, into the water. Drain 15 minutes more.

Remove the curds from the bag and refrigerate. The next day, add the baking soda and work it into the curd with your hands.

Place the curd in a heavy pan and bring to 180°F (82.2°C). Stir continuously. When the curds become translucent and smooth, pour into custard cups, or ramekins. Refrigerate for 24 hours.

After refrigerating, remove the cheese from the cups, and it is ready to eat.

Amish Cup Cheese Uses and Pairings

— — — — — — —

Serve this cheese with dark brown bread and stout coffee at breakfast to enjoy it as the Amish do. Amish cup cheese is also good on crackers or flatbreads.

Cottage Cheese

SOURCE: Sue Conley of Cowgirl Creamery.

One of the most versatile of cheeses, cottage cheese goes with almost everything.

INGREDIENTS

1 gallon nonfat milk
1 cup buttermilk
1 tray ice cubes

½ to 1 cup crème fraiche
Noniodized salt to taste

Cottage Cheese Uses and Pairings

———————

Cottage cheese with fresh fruit or over a sliced heirloom tomato is cool and refreshing in summer. In the cooler months, it goes well with heavier meats and stews. Try it with pastas, too.

For a special treat, drizzle your freshly made cottage cheese with honey and sprinkle with cinnamon.

Pour the milk into a sanitized cooking pot. Place the pot in a large bowl or larger stockpot and surround the milk pot with water at 90°F (32.2°C). With a sanitized spoon, stir in the buttermilk. Leave the milk in the water bath to incubate for 24 hours or until a firm, custardlike curd forms. The temperature of the milk will slowly decrease from 90°F to room temperature, or about 70°F (21°C).

With a long knife, cut the curd into smaller curds. First cut the curd, top to bottom, into slices ½ inch (13 mm) apart; then cut it again at right angles into ½-inch (13-mm) slices. Then, using the knife or a sanitized ladle, cut the curds horizontally at an angle from the bottom of the pot upward into ½-inch (13-mm) cubes. Leave undisturbed for 15 minutes.

Place the pot, still in the water bath, over medium heat and cook slowly until the curds and whey reach 120°F (48.9°C). The temperature should not rise more than one degree a minute, so this process will take up to 1 hour. (If you cook the curds too quickly, the outer skin of the curd will be too firm and the inside will be too mushy.) Stir gently just a few times until the temperature reaches 90°F (32.2°C), then stir constantly until it reaches 120°F (48.9°C).

Line a colander with cheesecloth and set it in the sink or over a large bowl. Using a perforated spoon, ladle the curds into the colander and let drain for 15 minutes.

Fill a large bowl with the ice cubes and some cold water. Remove the curds, still wrapped in the cheesecloth, from the colander and gather up the edges like a bag. Holding the cloth together so the curds stay inside, dip the bag into the ice water and swirl it around for about 5 minutes to wash off the curds. Return the curds, still in the cloth, to the colander and drain for 1 hour.

Place the curds in a sanitized bowl, add crème fraiche as desired, and stir. Season to taste with salt.

Cottage cheese can be stored if you cover it tightly and refrigerate. Use within one week.

Cream Cheese

Cream cheese has become a commodity product. Bring it back to life and make your own. It is a simple task, and nothing surpasses the announcement of "I made the cheese myself."

INGREDIENTS

1 gallon pasteurized whole goat or cow milk
¼ teaspoon Mesophilic DVI MA culture
3 drops of liquid rennet in 1/8 cup of nonchlorinated water
    (measure out 2 teaspoons of this mixture and discard the rest)
noniodized salt to taste

In a large cooking pot, warm the milk to 86°F (30°C). Add the culture, then the rennet solution (remember, only 2 teaspoons of the dilution). Cover the pot and allow it to sit at room temperature (70°F or 21°C) for 12 to 18 hours. It will have the appearance of yogurt.

Line a colander with cheesecloth, doubling the cloth to catch the curd, or use butter muslin (a finer cheesecloth). Ladle the curd into the colander and allow it to drain for about 12 hours. The best way to drain it is to hang the bag over the sink to allow the weight of the cheese to compress the curd.

After 12 hours, remove the cheese from the bag and work in the salt.

Refrigerate the cheese. When it is well chilled, you may make it into logs or blocks to resemble traditional cream cheese. Eat and enjoy.

Cream Cheese Uses and Pairings

Use this classic as you would the commercial variety—grilled on sandwiches, cut up in omelets, or blended into desserts. A favorite sandwich after Thanksgiving is a grilled turkey, avocado, and cream cheese affair. It doesn't even seem like leftovers!

Butter

One of the highlights of grade school was making butter. I remember my teacher bringing in cream in a quart jar. All the children sat in a circle and rolled the jar back and forth, and in a very short time we had butter! Since then I have made butter in a blender, a food processor, an antique churn, and an industrial churn. I have never lost my fascination with butter! I like to use the old butter paddles, available in antique stores, to work the butter, then press it into an old wooden mold. Don't forget to save the buttermilk! It's great for biscuits.

Butter requires heavy cream. Cow milk is the easiest milk to skim cream from. Goat milk has cream, too, but because of the nature of goat milk, this cream is more difficult to obtain. Often a cream separator is required to skim goat milk. Some people prefer to use a slightly soured cream for the milk, while others use fresh cream (known as sweet cream).

To separate the cream from fresh pasteurized cow milk, allow the milk to sit, refrigerated, overnight. You will observe a thick layer of cream on top of the milk. Using a large spoon or ladle, dip down into the cream, trying not to bring the milk back up with it. You may not be able to capture all the cream, but get as much as you can without disturbing the milk.

To churn cream into butter, use 1 pint of heavy cream. The temperature of the cream should be approximately 65°F (18.3°C). Put the cream in a quart jar, and shake or roll the jar back and forth for about 20 minutes. Flakes of butter will start to appear. If you have access to a churn, all the better, or use your blender. With the blender, butter will come in about 4 to 5 minutes. Simply turn the blender on a low setting, and you can watch the butter form; just scrape down the sides of the blender as it forms.

After the milk becomes butter, it is time to wash and gather the butter. Wash the small pieces of butter in cool water and then work them in a bowl with a butter paddle or large wooden spoon. Keep pressing the butter until all the buttermilk has been worked out. The buttermilk will make the butter sour quickly.

After this step has been accomplished, add salt to taste. Start with ½ teaspoon and see if that is right for you; if not add more—just work it into the butter.

Mold butter into a dish, sticks, or a wooden mold. After the butter keeps its shape, unmold and refrigerate. It will keep about a week.

Ricotta

This recipe for a whole-milk ricotta originates from Italy. It is rich, creamy, and filling. Ricotta was once primarily made from sheep milk. However, with industrialization of the process, cow-milk ricotta has become the norm even in Italy's creameries.

INGREDIENTS

1 gallon whole cow milk

½ cup apple-cider vinegar

1 tablespoon noniodized salt

Place milk in a large cooking pot over medium-low heat. Stir often to avoid any scorching. Bring the milk up to 190°F (87.7°C) and remove from heat.

Stir and add the vinegar while stirring. Tiny bits of curd will form.

Pour the curds into a cheesecloth-lined colander. Drain for about 30 minutes.

Add the salt, working it gently into the curds.

If you want a creamier texture, stir in 2 or 3 tablespoons of cream.

This cheese keeps about a week in the refrigerator.

Ricotta Uses and Pairings

Ricotta is frequently featured in lasagna and other pasta dishes, such as manicotti, as it marries perfectly with a zesty marinara sauce. And don't forget that ricotta can be sweetened to make a perfect filling for crepes.

Whey Ricotta

Whey is a great byproduct of cheesemaking. Rather than allowing the whey to simply go down the drain, save it. Animals such as pigs and chickens love it. It is good for the garden, too.

Or you can make a ricotta from leftover whey. It's a great way to make something from almost nothing! The whey does need to be fresh to make the cheese, though.

INGREDIENTS

2 gallons fresh whey

2 cups goat or cow milk

¼ cup apple-cider vinegar

½ teaspoon noniodized salt

Add the milk to the whey and heat to 190°F (87.7°C), stirring frequently to prevent scorching. Once you reach 190°F (87.7°C), turn off the heat and add the vinegar. Small curds will form at this point.

Ladle the curds into a cheesecloth-lined colander. Allow to drain several hours, then salt and refrigerate.

This cheese will keep about a week.

CHAPTER 2

Milk: The Cheesemaker's Palette

When milk is combined with the skill of the cheesemaker, the possibilities are endless. Nothing captures the heart of a region like cheese.

Cow, goat, sheep, yak, buffalo, and camel milk can all be used for making cheese. Even mare's milk has been used for cheesemaking by the truly adventurous. The most common milks for cheese in the United States are cow, goat, and sheep, respectively.

Milk is composed of water, lactose, protein, minerals, and fat. The level of butterfat in the milk will influence the final outcome of the cheese. Some cheeses call for lower fat levels, such as ricotta; others, such as triple cream brie, call for cream to be added to the milk.

Many do not realize milk is fragile. The actions of whipping, stirring, and beating change the structure of milk and break the fat cells into very small particles. Handle milk for cheesemaking with care.

Those who are fortunate enough to have a farm with their own animals will develop a preference for a particular species. Each species is known for specific attributes, such as high milk yields, the butterfat content of the milk, and temperament. A true bond forms between the dairyman or -woman and the animals. Milking is an intimate relationship based upon trust. Man and beast spend a great deal of time together, and each learns the other's habits. As in the human society, there are those with easygoing personalities, and then there are the high-maintenance creatures. Favorites develop, as well as a few who will exit the farm post haste, passed on to the next unsuspecting victim.

Food can capture the essence of a region; cheese can capture the heart of it. Milk, in a cheesemaker's hand, becomes as clay to a potter. It can be molded, formed into something totally new. A talented cheesemaker can literally bring a sense of place to your table, in the form of a wheel of perfectly aged cheese.

Terroir

Cheese is often described in terms similar to those used in characterizing wine. Expect to hear such terms as *acidic*, *mushroomy*, and *fruity*. A trained taster can pick up subtleties, such as hints of alfalfa or grass hay. As it does with wine, the region of production plays a large role in the final flavor of the cheese. The French

term *terroir* is somewhat ambiguous in our county. *Terroir* refers to the rationalities associated with production and takes in atmospheric conditions, terrain, and more. Terroir truly establishes a sense of place within a consumable product. The French are known for their recognition of place in their production. Perhaps you have experienced this sensation when eating a piece of fruit or drinking a glass of wine; it is almost as if you were there in the orchard or the vineyard, taking in the scenery, the scents, the textures, and the atmosphere. If these notes are captured within a particular vintage, be it wine or cheese, then the producer has achieved the ultimate goal. At this point, the making goes from production to art; for the maker, the status of a master of the craft soon follows.

Locale is another variable in milk production and the flavor of the resulting cheese. Cows in the Swiss Alps produce milk that has a different flavor profile that those producing in another location. Cow milk from Maine differs subtly from cow milk from California or Missouri. It is these subtleties that make cheese a regional food. If a cheesemaker in Vermont creates a cloth-bound cheddar, and a cheesemaker in another location does the same, there will be differences in flavor. The differences come from a variety of sources: the hand of the maker, the composition of the milk, the diet of the animals, the stage of lactation the animals were in, the aging conditions, humidity, overall climate, and other factors. This is where the art of the craft comes in to play.

Artisan-style cheesemakers understand seasonality and the varying palette they work with each day. Sometimes, slight changes are made in the make procedure to compensate for the changing milk supply. Some cheeses are only produced seasonally, others only in a particular region. In France, the *Appellation D'Origine Controlée* (A.O.C.) governs the production and naming of cheese, guarding trademarks and restricting the use of particular names to particular areas. For example, production of Crottin de Chavignol is controlled, and this cheese can only be

continued on page 50

Similarities in climatic conditions exist between one state and another, but there are specific elements of each state that create a unique environment. Terroir cannot be duplicated; it is not manmade. A cheesemaker in Missouri cannot make the same cheese as a cheesemaker in California. Those with a trained palate will detect subtle differences in cheese flavor due to the diet of the animal whose milk was used, the climate, the aging process, and, last but not least, the hand of the cheesemaker.

Tasha Tudor

I first learned of the late Tasha Tudor when I was looking for information on goats. I found a reference to her and her work and quickly became a fan. She was a strong and independent woman, ahead of her time in many ways, living her life centered around the best things of yesterday.

Tudor is well known within the genre of children's literature, having written such popular works as *Dorcus Porkus*, *A Time to Keep*, and *Becky's Christmas*. Tudor established herself early in life as an artist and a businesswoman. Her work centered around her home, her family, and her menagerie of animals. As a teenager, she saved to buy her first cow. The love affair began, and Tudor maintained dairy animals most of her life.

Tudor was enamored with things of the past. She preferred to live an austere and simple life that resembled daily life a century before her time. Handmade creations surrounded her, and family heirlooms were a part of her everyday life. Such tasks as candle making, weaving, gardening, and milking spun the fabric of daily activities of her home, Corgi Cottage, named for her constant companions, her Corgi dogs.

Her daughter-in-law, Marjorie Tudor, says, "When Tasha moved to Vermont, she had a cow. Tasha was always very slight, and one day the cow kicked her. She stated that was enough of that, and soon goats came to the farm. She needed the goats' milk for health reasons, and she was always quite fond of them. At one time she had seven! I believe she kept goats for at least twenty-five years." Tudor milked her goats twice a day, and Nubians were her preferred breed. She made cheese frequently.

Marjorie's husband, Seth, is Tasha's eldest son. He built her home and barn using only hand tools. In the New England custom, the barn is attached to the house in anticipation of cold winters and heavy snows. As Marjorie says, "In good weather, the goats had their own pen with a big fenced in area. It was nice, and they had a lot of rocks and boulders to play on. They did, however, kill all the trees! We frequently enjoyed goat's milk ice cream. We always made it in a hand-cranked freezer."

Tudor frequently added goats to the illustrations for her books and was able to capture her animals' unique and mischievous personalities. Perhaps these authentic likenesses came from her innate understanding of the animals and the fact that she knew each one so well. She also re-created other real-life elements in her work: The children she drew were her own her two sons and two daughters. Later, grandchildren became popular subjects. Marjorie says, "Tasha sketched all summer long. She mainly worked on her books in the winter. She was driven, and nothing stood in her way when she had a book to do. In addition to being an artist, she was an astute businesswoman."

Tudor, a true American icon, will long be remembered for her art, her stories, and her way of life. She was quoted as saying, "I've never had a headache. I have never been depressed. I attribute my long life to gardening and goat's milk." Perhaps there is a lesson in her words for us all. ◆

Beloved children's book illustrator--and pioneering artisan cheesemaker--Tasha Tudor. AP PHOTO/THE TUDOR FAMILY

A Missouri morning at an old homestead. The lush grass of the region is perfect for hay.

continued from page 47

made and called by that particular name in the hamlet of Chavignol. Such creations as Brie de Meausand and Brie du Melun are also A.O.C. recognized and controlled. Italy has similar controls. For the purposes of this book, cheese are designated by a style—as in, brie style, blue style, Italian style.

Other Factors Influencing Milk Flavor

Many factors influence the overall flavor of milk. Changes in the composition take place over the course of the animal's lactation cycle. Early spring milk is different than early winter milk. Changes in the animals' diet, as they go from summer grasses to winter hay, have quite an impact on flavor. Hot summer conditions can cause changes as well. Other factors, such the health, age, and even the breed of the animal, make a difference in the milk's final flavor profile.

Milk is not static. In fact, the chemistry of milk changes almost daily. The composition of this valuable liquid varies due to a number of factors. The first milk produced after an animal gives birth is called colostrum. This milk will not work for cheesemaking. It is rich and thick, yellow in color. This milk is meant for the newborn and contains vitamins and antibodies to get the youngster off to a good start. It takes about three days for this substance to turn into clear and true milk, as we know it. The milk will change throughout lactation due to hormonal and natural changes taking place within the milking animal's internal cycle.

The diet of the lactating animal has a tremendous impact upon the end flavor and quality of the milk. Milk from grass-fed animals is best. The cow, the goat, and the sheep were designed to eat vegetation—the fresher the better. It is only through domestication that this diet has changed. Humans have required the confinement of animals and the switch to feeding them concentrated foods.

The changes in milk present both a challenge and an opportunity in the making of cheese. As one progresses as a cheesemaker, these variances can be exploited, and various specialty products can come from seasonal production. Producing a limited-edition product, only available for a certain period of the year, can be, in fact, a covert marketing technique. Who does not want to buy the first and the last—the product that is in short supply—and get the bragging rights that accompany that purchase?

Milking and Handling

The milk-making process is one of supply and demand. If the milk is not taken by nursing offspring or by human means, the animal's supply will decrease and then stop until the birth of the next offspring. Milking time for the farmer is typically scheduled at twelve-hour intervals. This timing allows the milk supply to build up, and then its release stimulates the hormonal action to make more milk. If the milk is not taken, hormones send the message to decrease the supply. This decrease would happen naturally if the offspring were left to nurse with the mother, as newborns typically nurse for only the first three months of life. However, for the dairy farmer, production is key to profitability. The twelve-hour interval is a respected means of scheduling to keep the milk production high. Some large commercial dairies have implemented a three-times-per-day milking schedule. There is an increased output, but also higher labor costs, as more hands are needed to keep the milk line occupied.

The handling of the milk will also affect the end flavor. Dairy farmers clean, clean, and then clean some more to ensure a safe supply. In a commercial setting, animals entering the milking parlor are disinfected, wiped down, and tested for illness that might affect the quality of the milk. After the milk has been acquired, chilling begins immediately. Remember that bacterial-replication cycle. For commercial producers, milk is piped directly from the milking station to a refrigerated bulk tank. It's also important that the milk be handled gently. Excess foaming can damage the delicate cells and change the composition of the milk drastically. Dairies are inspected frequently and fall under the governing body of the U. S. Department of Agriculture.

A pair of Jersey cows.

continued on page 55

Vermont Shepherd

At Vermont Shepherd, milking takes place in the milking parlor. The barn, over 200 years old, is a spectacular piece of architecture and the heart of the farm. Constructed of wood from the now-extinct American chestnut, this centerpiece of the farm was originally built as a dairy barn for cows. Owner David Major made a few structural changes to accommodate the sheep.

David Major begins this day as he has begun many others, by tending to his flock. Accompanied by a faithful dog or two, he escorts his milking ewes to the pasture after milking and resets the electrified netting used to contain the sheep. The dogs—a Pyrenees, a Maremma, and a border collie—assist David in moving the sheep from barn to pasture. The dogs are also the main means of predator control on the farm.

David's fondness for his flock is evident as he watches over them in the valley, "Every group has a leader. They know their routine." He calls to them, "Come by, come by," and all 159 heads turn to heed his voice.

David and his wife, Yesenia, are the farmers behind Vermont Shepherd, a successful sheep dairy known for artisan-style cheese.

David grew up on his parents' farm just down the road, where sheep were the central focus. "At one time wool was a profitable venture. We raised Dorsets and between the market price for the wool and the government subsidies, it was possible to make

Sheep on their way to pasture at Vermont Shepherd. These crossbreed animals are quite hardy and able to survive in the extreme Vermont winters. The sheep are pulled into the barn during the coldest times of the year, for lambing. Sheep milk is quite viscous due to the high fat content. Wool is a secondary product in the dairy-sheep industry. The Majors offer handspun wool in their farm store.

a living from the sheep," he says. However, things changed: the government incentives ceased, and the price paid for wool dropped, too. David began to look for other ways to continue in the sheep business and make a living at the same time.

"We began to experiment with milking the sheep," he recalls. "We brought in a Tunas ram and started breeding with milk production in mind. Our first cheese was horrible. There was no training for cheesemaking here in the States when we began. We learned trial by error."

As luck would have it, a college student from France came to intern on the farm and an exchange began. "We were invited to France and stayed with our student's family. We were only there for two weeks, but after three years of struggling, we knew what questions to ask," David says.

Yesenia, originally from the Dominican Republic, also came from a heritage rich in agricultural pursuits. "I know what hard work is. We farm in the Dominican Republic," she says. Yesenia fell in love with the Vermont countryside and the routines of farm life. "If farming doesn't give you reason to live, I don't know what would. It all has to do with planting the seed or seeds being planted," she says.

The Vermont Shepherd sheep follow a rotational grazing system. The pasture contains a natural blend of grasses; orchard; blue, red, and white clover; and narrow-leaf plantain. David explains, "You can pick up on the notes of the various grasses in the cheese. The pasture becomes a part of the cheese."

David Major is one of the primary leaders in the dairy-sheep industry in the United States. "We were the first sheep dairy," he says modestly. An inventor and innovator, he created a small pipeline in the farm's dairy to direct the milk into a central collection can. He also has become known in the industry for his stanchions, which keep the animals in place for milking.

From the milk parlor, the milk is transported into the cheese house. The milk is cultured and renneted according to the season. Sheep milk has varying levels of solids during the lactation cycle, and David has learned to work with the natural elements of the milk to create a consistent cheese.

The cheese produced on the farm is appropriately named Vermont Shepherd. A full-bodied tomme, a mountain cheese with a washed rind, is aged in a nearby cellar snuggled into the earth. Fresh, raw-milk cheese is transported to the cellar, or

The aging facility at Vermont Shepherd is a manmade cave tucked back into a hillside near the farm. Climate controlled for temperature and humidity, it is the storehouse for a year's production of cheese.

The treasure trove of Vermont Shepherd. Each wheel is marked with the distinctive brand of the sheep and the number of each make. Ash is the preferred wood for the shelving.

cave, and placed there for aging for three to six months. Each wheel is numbered and marked with the imprint of the sheep.

The cheese is moved through the cellar following a course of ash boards carefully selected for the purpose of aging. The cheese is carefully washed in a brine solution and then moved through the chamber in a specified progression. Yesenia explains, "It is turned twice a week and then moved through the cave." The natural rind develops during the aging process, and the unique flavor, texture, and essence of the cheese is purely a Vermont farmstead creation.

Eager customers await the end of the aging process, and the cheese is sold as soon as it becomes available. "We usually sell out in February, and we don't have any available again until August. We currently produce about 20,000 pounds [90,718 kg] per year," says David. Most of the cheese is sold through wholesale markets, and the demand exceeds the supply—a goal all cheese producers hope to achieve.

David and Yesenia maintain relationships with their local customers with a small on-farm store. "It is good for the community, and it gives people an excuse to come to the farm," David says. At the farm store, neighbors can purchase cheese, yarn spun from Vermont Shepherd sheep, locally made sheep-milk soap, maple syrup harvested by David's brother, and other local favorites, such as mint tea. Customers fill out a slip listing their purchases and leave their payments in a box.

David and Yesenia have gone back to her family farm in the Dominican Republic and shared some of their cheesemaking techniques with her family.

Yesenia reports, "They now have a market for their milk. They make cheese and transport it by donkey to two neighboring villages. Sometimes they laugh at the things we do, but they cannot deny that each time we go back, we are stronger and healthier. We look better and feel better. It all comes from the farm, from this way of life. . . . You are either a part of it, or you're not. The proof is in the pudding"—and in the cheese! ♦

The sign at the Vermont Shepherd farm store sets the tone for the neighborhood shop. The sign is a reminder of days gone, by when commerce was conducted on an individual basis. Neighbors stop in and purchase cheese, handmade soap (made from the farm's sheep milk), yarn spun from the farm's wool, and maple syrup. The cash box is a wooden affair with a slit in the top. Customers figure their own tab and leave a check. "We've never had a problem," says owner David Major.

The Vermont Shepherd farm store: a cozy spot with cheese in the refrigerator, waiting for the neighborhood shopper. "We like this store and offering our products directly to our neighbors," says owner David Major.

continued from page 51

Cow Milk

Cows remain the primary source for milk in North America, and the **Holstein** is the most common of the dairy breeds.

The Holstein and **Friesian** are easily recognized by their distinctive black-and-white coloration. Heavy producers, these breeds of cow produce an average of 3,260 gallons of milk per lactation cycle. The butterfat content is about 2.5 to 3 percent.

The **Jersey** is another well-known breed. Smaller in stature than the Holstein, the Jersey produces milk that is good for making cheese. Average production of a Jersey cow is 1,860 gallons per lactation cycle, and its milk has a significantly higher butterfat content—4.9 percent—than that of the Holstein.

The **Guernsey** breed originated in the British Isles. A small cow, the Guernsey produces an average of 1,700 gallons per lactation cycle, and the milk has a significant butterfat content of 4.5 percent.

The **Brown Swiss** breed is believed to have originated in the Swiss Alps. Hardy animals with high production rates, they average 2,450 gallons per lactation cycle, and their milk is 4 percent butterfat.

Fresian and Holstein cows graze in the shade of a massive pasture tree. Holsteins are a hardy breed and can withstand weather extremes. Undoubtedly when people hear the word cow, *this breed, with its distinctive coloration, comes to mind.*

Goat Milk

Goats, while much maligned, are fabulous animals. They adapt well to land unfit for other agricultural endeavors, converting brush and otherwise unusable plant materials into milk.

There are many myths surrounding goats. The primary myth is that goats will eat anything. Goats are, in fact, picky eaters. They will eat grass only if they have no other choice. They will not eat soiled hay or drink dirty water. Nor will they eat tin cans; I believe this misconception became a common belief when someone saw a goat either eating the label off of a can or licking the inside of it for sugar and salt, which goats enjoy.

Goats can eat a variety of plants that cause grief for the farmer. A goat will thoroughly enjoy problematic plants such as poison ivy, wild rosebushes, thistle, and other problem-causing growth. Many farmers employ a herd of "brush goats" specifically for this purpose. Often farmers will run goats with cattle to eat the brush the cows won't touch. This arrangement works quite well.

Goats have interesting personalities. Some are sweet and loving; others

An Alpine dairy goat, looking wise beyond her years. The following colorations are standard for the Alpine breed: Cou blanc, literally "white neck," has white front quarters and black hindquarters with black or gray markings on the head. Cou clair, "clear neck" means front quarters are tan, saffron, off white, or shading to gray and black hindquarters. Cou noir, "black neck," indicates black front quarters and white hindquarters. Sundgau means black with white markings. Pied indicates mottled coloring. Chamoisee animals are brown or bay colored.

adopt the lead goat mentality and let everyone know who's the real boss. These animals thrive on routine and are upset by change. Milking for goats is the same as for cows: twice a day at twelve-hour intervals for the highest yields. A grade (which is an unregistered animal) produces about one gallon of milk per day.

There are six breeds recognized by the American Dairy Goat Association. The **Saanen** is a beautiful all-white goat and the highest yielding of the six breeds.

The **Nubian** is known for its long ears and roman nose. Nubian milk is typically higher in butterfat and protein than that of other breeds.

The **LaMancha** is a funny little creature with tiny ears that resemble human ears. These goats are good producers and have gentle temperaments.

The **Alpine** can be almost any color except solid white or light brown with white markings. Their face is straight with erect ears. They are large producers.

The **Oberhaslis** has specific color standards. They are a bay color, known as chamoise, with a black dorsal strip, udder, and belly; they are black below the knees and have nearly black heads. Does may be all black.

The **Toggenburg** breed has a specific color requirement of light brown with white ears and white lower legs. The dies of the tail and two stripes down the face must also be white. They have erect ears and have the smallest height requirement of all the breeds.

Goat milk, if handled properly, does not have a goaty flavor. Probably the number one complaint regarding goat milk is just that, a goaty flavor. Certain situations, including unclean milking conditions, unclean animals, a buck in the same area as the does, and delayed chilling of milk can allow this off taste to develop.

Goat milk contains **caprylic acid**. This acid is specific to goat milk and gives the milk a distinctive tang. Some cheesemakers capitalize upon it,

Ask any goat farmer about the primary challenge in raising these animals, and he or she will speak of fencing. Goats are surely related to Harry Houdini when it comes to being escape artists. Good fencing relieves a lot of problems. Goats love flowers, shrubs, and gardens. Someone once said, "Goats are like people: they like to eat out at least once a week." Any goat farmer will attest to this fact.

and the desired cheese is meant to have that distinctive bite. However, many of the mild cheeses or the fresh varieties will have a light tang without the strong flavor. For those who have not enjoyed goat cheese before, it is good to start with the mild varieties.

Sheep Milk

Sheep milk has long been utilized by the cheesemakers of the world. This milk is low in water content and high in fat—actually, about two times higher in fat when compared to cow milk. This high fat content makes milking sheep worth the effort. Though the yield of milk is quite low, ranging from a pint to two quarts, depending on the breed, the fat content is so high that the volume of whey produced is cut drastically. Less whey equals more curd, or solid, production. The price of sheep-milk cheese outweighs that of cow-milk cheese; sheep-milk products reportedly sell for four times the price of cow-milk products.

Sheep are willing participants in the milking process. Trained to follow particular patterns, they look forward the feed associated with milking time. Sheep are fed carefully calculated rations to ensure a slow, but steady milk supply. Unfortunately, these animals are largely defenseless and, if left to their own devices, would perish quickly. Guard animals serve as protectors and herd masters. The Great Pyrenees is a breed of massive white dogs that are often placed in the role of watchman. Border collies work the sheep, bringing them to and fro at their master's command. A border collie working its flock is a joy to behold. Responding to whistles, hand signals, or voice commands, these dogs are quick-witted and masterful beasts. Llamas, donkeys, and other dog breeds are also employed as herd guardians. Even with protection, loss to predators is a constant concern for sheep producers.

In addition to producing milk, the dairy breeds of sheep bear wool and require shearing annually. Shepherds report the value of their wool is low and often does not cover the cost of a shearer. Most sheep operations will also sell lamb, a favorite for Easter dinner and various holiday celebrations.

Sheep milk lends itself well to the creation of feta, ricotta, and pecorino romano. Roquefort is also typically made of sheep milk. Flavor profiles vary greatly, and some sheep-milk cheese is described as woolly or earthy. Aging brings out the more subtle characteristics, such as grass and lanolin notes.

Across the globe, sheep are well known as a milk-producing animal. European cheesemakers have long known of the virtues of sheep milk. However, the dairy breeds are relatively new to the United States, and only a small number were initially imported into this county. East Friesian is the most common dairy sheep breed in the United States; the breed originated in Germany. Friesians are considered to be the world's highest-milk-producing dairy sheep.

The Doolan-VanVlaanderen family enjoy a morning with the goats. The natural rock outcroppings are a favorite gathering spot for the family, and the goats enjoy the "high places." GREGORY J. LAMOUREUX

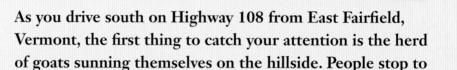

Does' Leap

A signature leaping doe is present on all Does' Leap products. Branding is important for all cheesemakers, whether you are creating products for friends or running a cheese operation. Make each product carry your signature in some way; design your own label, your own wrap—something that is distinctively you!

As you drive south on Highway 108 from East Fairfield, Vermont, the first thing to catch your attention is the herd of goats sunning themselves on the hillside. People stop to photograph the herd, which are oblivious to their admirers.

For Kristan Doolan and George VanVlaanderen, goats are a part of daily life. At Does' Leap, the couple has been producing their artisan-style cheese for more than nine years. Their creations include fresh chèvre, feta, caprella with a bloomy rind, a Trappist-style tomme, and kefir.

Doolan had a pet goat as a young girl, and when the couple began to consider a dairy, goats seemed to be a natural fit.

"We like the animals and their personalities. They are a manageable size. We now have a herd of fifty, mostly Alpine or Alpine Nubian crosses. We have spent the last nine years honing in on good genetics. Our herd is closed, and we are very happy being the size we are. We are living the dream," VanVlaanderen reports.

In the beginning, Doolan was the primary cheesemaker, while VanVlaanderen worked off the farm as a high school teacher. In 2007, he gave up his day job to devote his time to the farm. Now Does' Leap has one employee who takes care of the cheesemaking chores, as Doolan and VanVlaanderen both prefer doing the outdoor work.

As a part of their goat-herd management, Doolan and VanVlaanderen introduce draft and pleasure horses into the paddocks after the goats have moved to the next rotation. The horses are "dead-end hosts" for most of the parasites that are a problem for many goat herds. The horses are also used to work in the fields, cultivating the ground, mowing hay, and bringing in sap from the maples. Pigs also play a role in the farm operation. "The pigs are fed the whey from our cheesemaking," Doolan says. "They help us to reclaim previously unusable ground as they work it up, and our end product is whey-fed pork. The pigs help us add several thousand dollars a year to our sales and solve a problem of what to do with the whey."

The goats are moved through a series of pastures as a part of a managed rotational-grazing system. Explains VanVlaanderen, "They go to a fresh paddock every twelve hours. Sometimes we move them several times a day, depending on the grass." Guard dogs provide predator control and watch the goats twenty-four hours a day.

"Our [cheese] market is 99 percent local now," says VanVlaanderen. "In the beginning, we were shipping cheese as far away as California. However, our customer base in Burlington [Vermont] sustains us now. We have a following. The biggest thing we do, as far as marketing, is to have people taste our cheese. The increasing demand for local, artisan products has had an impact on our sales, and we definitely have a group of customers wed to our cheese. We have developed our aged cheeses so we have product and a market year round."

When asked what advice she has for aspiring dairy farmers and cheesemakers, Doolan says, "[I]t is tough, financially, to make it work. Expect at least twelve hours a day, seven days a week. Some have a very romantic vision of cheesemaking and farming, in general." She adds, "We didn't come upon this overnight. Some things have worked; others have not. Be prepared for two or three years of suffering. It takes awhile, but there is beauty in selling your own products." ♦

Kristan Doolan expertly drives the majestic team. The horses serve many purposes on the farm: Guardians, muscle power, and parasite management. As George says, "We couldn't run the farm without them.
GREGORY J. LAMOUREUX

Devonshire Cream

SOURCE: Inspired by and adapted from Carla Emery's recipe in her *Encyclopedia of Country Living*

Traditional Devonshire cream is popular in England. This is a clotted cream—rich, sweet, and decadent. It is also quite expensive to buy! This recipe makes a delicious Devonshire cream, and I recommend that you have lots of milk and cream to play with.

I am a long-time fan of Carla Emery and her *Encyclopedia of Country Living*. I learned a great deal of my country skills with her book in one hand and a goat in the other. Emery lives on through her wonderful literary work. This recipe is an adaptation of Carla's.

INGREDIENTS

2 quarts milk
1 quart heavy cream

Combine the milk and cream in a mixing bowl and refrigerate for 12 hours.

Place the milk and cream mixture into a heavy pot and heat to 90°F (32°C). Hold at this temperature for 3 to 5 hours. To do this, you may use a double boiler and add hot water as needed to maintain the temperature. A second method of maintaining the temperature is to place the cooking pot in a sink of hot water and add hot water as needed. The milk will develop a thick layer on top. Do not disturb this layer.

Refrigerate again for 12 hours.

The next day, skim off the thick top layer, and it's ready to eat.

Devonshire Cream Uses and Pairings

Nothing tops a fresh scone like Devonshire cream. Try it with fresh fruits, too. Fresh strawberries and Devonshire cream are the perfect end to a summer supper.

Halloumi

SOURCE: Nancy Micheal of Cairo, Egypt

Halloumi is a staple in Egypt. It is a classic cheese made with what is on hand and requires no special equipment for pressing.

My friend Nancy Micheal lived in the city in Cairo. She farmed on her balcony, raising pigeons, rabbits, and vegetables high above the cityscape. To make her halloumi, she would frequently travel to the countryside for fresh milk.

Halloumi Uses and Pairings

This cheese is excellent when fried. Halloumi resists melting, and it is good on a vegetable kabob with yellow, green, and red peppers, mushrooms, and onions. It's also good when brined; see the accompanying recipe.

INGREDIENTS

2 quarts fresh goat or cow milk
½ teaspoon liquid rennet dissolved in ¼ cup nonchlorinated water
noniodized salt to taste

Heat the milk to 86°F (30°C). Add the rennet and allow to rest for 30 minutes.

Test for a clean break. When a clean break is achieved, cut the curds into 1-inch (25.5-mm) cubes. Place the curds in a colander lined with cheesecloth and allow to drain for about an hour. Make sure to reserve the whey!

Return the whey to the cooking pot and bring it to a boil. Remove the curds from the cheesecloth and cook them in the boiling whey until they float, about 15 minutes. Then place the curds back in the cheesecloth-lined colander. When all the curds are finished cooking and in the colander, remove them, still wrapped in the cloth. Fold the cloth over to make a pouch and then place the pouch on a dinner plate. Cover with another plate and add some weight—a brick covered with aluminum foil is perfect. Drain the whey every 5 minutes and continue to press for an hour.

After pressing, add salt to the exterior of the cheese and rub it in. Then refrigerate the cheese for at least an hour before serving.

Halloumi in Brine

Make halloumi as directed, but do not salt. Instead, make a fully saturated brine. Add 2 sliced green peppers to the brine; the green peppers add a subtle flavor to the cheese. Press the cheese as directed above, then cut it into 3 x 3-inch (7.6 x 7.6-cm) cubes. Place the cubes in the brine and leave for 12 hours. The cheese will be salty from the brine, so wash off the extra brine and dry the cubes. It is then ready to eat.

Feta

Inspired by Molly Nolte of Fias Co Farm

Feta originated in Greece, where it was traditionally made of sheep milk. It is now common to use cow or goat milk. The salty brine is the trademark of this cheese. It is lightly pressed to allow the structure of the cheese to remain open, so the brine penetrates the interior as well as the exterior of the cheese.

Molly Nolte of Fias Co Farm is well known for her extensive website full of valuable information on animal husbandry and other homestead topics. This is Molly's recipe for her famous feta. She usually makes her feta from raw, unpasteurized goat milk.

The lipase powder is the enzyme that gives feta that great flavor. It is not vegetarian; you can omit it if you wish, but the resulting cheese will not have as much flavor. Molly uses kid/lamb lipase because she likes a strong feta flavor.

Feta Uses and Pairings

– – – – – –

Feta is often highlighted in dishes created with the Greek classic, phyllo dough. Use feta in such favorites as spanakopita (spinach pie). Feta also holds its own in a Greek salad.

INGREDIENTS

2 gallons sheep, goat, or cow milk
¼ teaspoon Mesophilic DVI MA culture
¼ teaspoon kid/lamb lipase powder
1 teaspoon liquid rennet dissolved in ½ cup nonchlorinated water
kosher salt

BRINE INGREDIENTS

½ cup kosher salt per ½ gallon of water (boiled and cooled down to room temperature)

In a double boiler, warm the goat milk to 86°F (30°C) or the cow milk to 88°F (31°C). Remove from heat. Add the culture and the lipase. Stir well and let ripen, covered, for 1 hour.

Add the rennet and stir briskly for 15 seconds. Cover and let set 30 to 40 minutes or until you get a clean break.

After a clean break is achieved, cut the curd into ½-inch (13-mm) strips. Then turn the pot 90 degrees and cut across in ½-inch (13-mm) slices in the other direction, making a checkerboard pattern. Now hold the knife at a sideways, 45-degree angle and retrace your cuts. Turn the pot a quarter turn and retrace the cuts. Turn it again and cut. And then one final turn and cut. By the last turn, you probably won't be able to see the original cuts, but just do the best you can. If you don't think you cut the curd perfectly, don't worry. Let the curds rest—10 minutes for goat milk, 5 minutes for cow milk.

After this rest period, stir the curd gently and cut any pieces that you missed when you first cut the curd. Hold the goat-milk curd at 86°F (30°C), or the cow-milk curd at 88°F (31°), for 45 minutes; keeping the pot covered will maintain the temperature. Check the temperature of the curds; if the temperature falls, place the pot in a sink full of 86°F (30°C) water to elevate the temperature of the curds and whey. Stir occasionally to prevent the curds from sticking together. This process of cooking the curd helps the curd to toughen up and the whey to release.

Place a colander over a large pot and line the colander with a large piece of fine cheesecloth. If the cheesecloth is dampened, it will stick slightly to the colander and be held in place. Carefully pour the curd into the colander. Tie the corners of the cheesecloth together and hang the bag to drain. Save the whey to make ricotta later.

After 3 to 4 hours, take the cheese down and turn it over, top to bottom. Move the cheese to a different piece of medium-weave cheesecloth. This turning will even up the cheese into a nice form. Flip the cheese and continue draining for about 24 hours.

At this point, the cheese will start to develop a distinctive odor. After the cheese has hung for about 24 hours, remove it from the cloth and cut it into usable, 2-inch (5-cm) cubes. Sprinkle all sides of the curds with kosher salt and place them in a sterilized, sealable container. Cover and let sit at room temperature for 2 to 3 days to harden up the blocks. The blocks will continue to release whey during this time.

Transfer the blocks to a large sterilized glass container, such as a glass pickle jar, and add the brine. If you add the brine too soon, the cheese sometimes starts to soften. If this happens, pour off the brine. The cheese is still good and can be used for cooking instead of crumbling.

Age the cheese in the brine for 1 to 4 weeks before use. The feta will keep up to a year if refrigerated.

Feta in Olive Oil with Sun-Dried Tomatoes

One of my students, Tanya Paul, is a wonderful cheesemaker. She brought this cheese to me as a gift.

Make the feta as in the previous recipe. Brine for 1 month, then remove 8 to 12 cubes. Place the cubes in a pint jar. Add onion slices, garlic cloves, sun-dried tomatoes, and fresh basil leaves. Arrange the basil leaves around the outside of the jar, so they look attractive; layer the cheese with the sliced onions, garlic, and tomatoes. Fill the jar with olive oil, and refrigerate for a few days for the flavors to blend. Serve at room temperature. The oil will pick up the flavors and makes an excellent salad dressing or dip for warm french bread.

Marinated Feta Uses and Pairings

– – – – –

Feta marinated in olive oil with sun-dried tomatoes is excellent on toasted bread or in a salad. Use the oil as a marinade.

Basket Cheese

SOURCE: Ricki Carroll of New England Cheesemaking Supply

In Italy, it is common to see cheese molded in reed baskets. The basket weavers still make the traditional cheese baskets. Although plastic has become widely used, nothing can replace the charm of the handwoven reed baskets. Whether made from reed or plastic, the baskets promote airflow and drainage, and they add a decorative pattern to the cheese.

SPECIAL EQUIPMENT
Basket molds

INGREDIENTS
1 gallon milk
¼ teaspoon rennet dissolved in ¼ cup non-chlorinated water
2 pinches noniodized salt

Heat the milk to 86 to 90°F (30 to 32°C) and add the rennet. Turn off the heat and let set for about 40 minutes.

After the milk has set, turn the heat back on low and heat again for about 2 minutes.

Using a slotted spoon, pull the curds to the side of the pot. Keep moving the curds for about 10 minutes with the slotted spoon. This breaks up the curd and keeps them draining.

Remove the curds from the pot with a slotted spoon and place them into a cheesemaker's basket or colander. Return the basket with the curds in it to the whey and cover the curds with the whey, pressing the curds into the basket with your hands.

Remove the basket from the whey. Set another mold inside of the first one and put a glass of water on top of it. This glass of water is used as a weight for pressing the cheese. Press by leaving the full glass of water on top of the cheese for 2 hours.

Take the cheese out of the basket. Turn it over, salt it to taste, return it to the basket, and continue pressing for 1½ hours longer. Remove the cheese from the basket and refrigerate.

This cheese has a three-day shelf life.

Basket Cheese Uses and Pairings

Try basket cheese on bruschetta or toast, drizzled with olive oil and topped with a pinch of garlic salt and a slice of ripe tomato—all paired with a bottle of chianti or other hearty Italian red. The depth and spicy nature of the wine pairs perfectly with this cheese.

Sainte Maure

SOURCE: Fias Co Farm

Once you have making chèvre down, why not try something really fun that gets moldy? And once you try this moldy chèvre, you may never go back to plain chèvre again.

We will make the chèvre recipe from Chapter 1 and add Penicillum candidum as a secondary culture. This mold is the same kind of white mold used in Brie and Camembert. It will grow to blanket the chèvre.

Sainte Maure is named for the region of France in which it was originally made—Ste. Maure de Touraine. This cheese is typically made in a log. French cheesemakers add a straw through the center of the cheese, largely to assist with handling, as it is quite delicate.

SPECIAL EQUIPMENT
Small cheese molds
1-gallon-size zip-top plastic bags
Aging mats

INGREDIENTS
1 gallon pasteurized goat milk
⅛ teaspoon Mesophilic DVI MA culture
⅛ teaspoon Penicillum candidum (Neige)
2 drops of liquid rennet dissolved in ¼ cup nonchlorinated water
noniodized salt

Sainte Maure Uses and Pairings

— — — — — — —

This cheese may be consumed fresh or aged for two to three weeks. It is the perfect cheese for dessert and pairs well with a light rosé wine.

Pour the goat milk into a cooking pot. Heat milk slowly to 86°F (30°C). Remove from heat.

Sprinkle the culture and white mold powder over the top of the milk and gently stir, making sure they are dissolved and well integrated into the milk. Allow this mixture to sit for about 45 minutes, so the culture has time to develop.

Add the rennet mixed in water and stir, coming up from the bottom of the pot, until the culture and rennet are well integrated into the milk. Let the mixture rest, covered with a cloth, in a warm place for 12 to 18 hours. The gel will thicken to the consistency of yogurt while it is resting.

Gently ladle the curds into a cheesecloth-lined colander and allow the curds and whey to drain for 2 hours. During this time, a great deal of the whey will drain away from the curd. Scoop the curd gently into cheese molds. (Use the small mold, such as the one for a crottin.) Allow the cheese to sit in the molds for 12 hours, then remove. To remove the cheese, run a butter knife around the edge of the cheese to loosen. Turn the mold upside down and rap the bottom of the mold with the palm of your hand. The cheese will dislodge from the mold. When you unmold the cheese, it may already have started to develop its fuzz.

Allow it to sit at room temperature for several hours, then place the cheese in a fully saturated salt brine for 10 minutes. Air dry for 2 hours, then place the cheese in an aging bag. Allow the curd to drain for about 12 hours. Then remove the curd from the aging bag, place it in a bowl, and work in the salt.

To age your Sainte Maure, place it on a drying mat cut smaller than a large, gallon-size, zip-top freezer bag. Slip the mat with the cheese into a bag, blow up the bag, and seal it. Now you have a little aging cave. I let my cheeses age on the counter for a few more days and then move them into my fridge. Here they continue to fuzz up for a few weeks.

You can eat your little fuzzies at any time, but try to let them age a couple weeks, if you can wait that long.

Goat-Milk Ice Cream

Small ice cream freezers have revolutionized homemade ice cream. Now, by keeping a frozen canister in the freezer, ice cream is only a short time away! These recipes are for a four-cup freezer; multiply for larger quantities.

INGREDIENTS
2 cups pasteurized goat milk
½ cup pure maple syrup

Blend these two ingredients together. Freeze and enjoy. Yield 3 cups of ice cream.

CHAPTER 3
Culture and Rennet

From milk or cream to cheese:

The catalyst is in the culture.

What makes cheese cheese? Why isn't cheese just sour milk? There are two components that basically make the difference: culture and rennet. Culture and rennet are what make the cheese world go round.

The Culture of Culture

There are some basic cheesemaking methods that simply allow milk to sour, such as the process used to make clabbered milk cheese. However, if a cheesemaker wants to go beyond that (and most do), then the proper environment must be created. That is exactly what culture does: it creates a hospitable environment, within the milk, to make cheese. Culture is basically beneficial bacteria. These bacteria replicate and create a hospitable environment for further replication while keeping unwanted bacterial growth in check. Culture also increases acidity, and acidity is crucial to cheesemaking. Finally, culture adds flavor.

Italian cheesemakers still use wooden vessels to create their cheese. Time and reuse of their vessels has infused that wood with bacteria all its own. If those cheesemakers were to be unable to use those same troughs for cheesemaking, surely something would be lost. That vessel or trough has become a part of the cheese, and the cheese is a part of that vessel.

In the United States, law prevents such an exchange. Cheesemaking in this country is largely clinical, due to laws governing food production. Therefore, a supplemental implantation of bacteria becomes an essential part of cheesemaking here.

A large part of commercial production relies on predictability. As a consumer, one expects to go to the grocer and buy the same product time and time again. If the product is not the same, disappointment soon follows. A mozzarella is expected to melt, cheddar is expected to be of a certain sharpness, and a Brie is expected to be molten at ripeness. These characteristics do not happen by accident, and the addition of prepared cultures to milk assists in creating the anticipated outcome. As a home cheesemaker, you will strive for the same goal: predictability. If you create a perfect product once, you will hope for the same outcome the next time you make it.

Those with an interest in cheesemaking will hear various terms when learning about culture. A **mother culture** is essentially a **starter culture** that must be cared for and developed.

In contrast, a **direct set**, or **direct vat innoculant (DVI)** culture, is ready to be added to the milk. With the development of a mother culture, there is great room for error and a certain risk in the development of the bacteria, as without the proper incubation conditions the bacteria will not be viable. For the purposes of making cheese at home, the easiest route is to use DVI cultures.

There are two basic types of DVI cultures:

Thermophylic (MM) are heat-loving bacteria and are used for pasta fillata or Italian-type cheeses, such as mozzarella, romano, reggiano, and taleggio. Thermophillic cultures are for cheeses which require high termpatures, typically Italian-style cheeses.

Mesophilic (MA) prefer cooler temperatures. This type of culture cannot survive the high temperatures required for the pasta fillata–type cheeses. Mesophilics are used for the creation of cheddars, goudas, chèvres, soft cheeses, and more. Mesophilic cultures are for low-temperature cheesemaking.

Cultures are available in two basic formats: frozen or freeze dried. Frozen cultures are usually available only in large quantities and require special temperatures to maintain, so the home cheesemaker will be more interested in the freeze-dried type. And there are two formats of freeze-dried cultures available. The first is a **concentrated type**, or a **mother** or **starter**. Again, the development of the

continued on page 76

Using Culture

Cultures look much like powdered milk. Our modern freeze-dried types are grown in a sterile environment, setting the stage for that repeatable format for making cheese.

In the make procedures listed, the culture is added to the milk and allowed to ripen for thirty to forty-five minutes. This time period allows for the development of the culture. During this time, it will multiply and **ripen** the milk.

Cultures need to be handled with great care, so the powder isn't contaminated. Paper clip the top of the pouch closed after use, then place the pouch in a plastic zip-top bag and keep it refrigerated. Take great care to use a clean measuring spoon each time, so the culture remains true to form.

When adding culture, bring the milk to the temperature specified in the make procedure. Be sure to remove the cooking pot from the heat source. With a sanitized measuring spoon, measure out the culture in the amount specified. Sprinkle this on top of the warm milk. Stir the culture into the milk with a slotted spoon, bringing milk up from the bottom of the pot to make sure the powder is thoroughly dissolved and well integrated into the milk. Do not whip or beat the milk. Stir for a full minute.

After this point, cover the pot with a clean towel or cheesecloth. Keep the pot in a draft-free place, maintaining the temperature. After the time specified in the recipe elapses, the milk is considered to be ripened. It is now time to add the rennet.

Sarah Hoffman, co-owner of Green Dirt Farm, in her element. Her custom cheese room was designed with the assistance of Neville McNaughton (see profile in Chapter 6). The layout of the make room is important to the flow of work and overall efficiency of the process. Cheesemaking is labor intensive, and every step saved matters. SARA FARRAR

Green Dirt Farm

As dawn breaks over the hills of northern Missouri, business partners Sarah Hoffman and Jacque Smith are already at work. With a milking herd of sheep numbering seventy-plus, the two women always have plenty tasks to accomplish.

Smith moves through the milk parlor, in her element, taking careful notes on the overall appearance, health, and milk production of each animal. Ever the shepherd, she keeps close watch on the flock. The milk parlor is immaculate, and it is quite obvious everyone, including the sheep, know their roles. Entering twelve at a time, the animals line up in their stalls at the stanchion, anticipating the grain that will enter the shoot. Munching happily, they have no qualms about sharing their milk. They keep a watchful eye on Mae, the well-trained border collie, awaiting the dog's commands.

Currently the yield is seven total gallons per milking. Due to the high fat content of sheep milk, the yield is about 20 percent milk to fresh cheese, 18 percent for aged cheese. At Green Dirt Farm, the sheep are 100 percent grass fed. There are no antibiotics, no hormones, no pesticides, and no confinement.

"I had some understanding of farm life," Smith says, describing how her family spent a lot of time gardening and shared a hobby farm with her aunts and uncles. "In college, I started to become more aware of our local

Jacque Smith, co-owner of Green Dirt Farm, is a one-woman show in the milking parlor. The sheep respond quickly, filing into the milking parlor and taking their turns in the stanchion. The milking system includes a pipeline that sends the milk to a central collection tank. From there, the milk is pumped into the cheese room and the vats. SARA FARRAR

food system and the importance of creating a culture focusing on local foods. At that time, there were only a handful of farmers who were trying to create such a culture here in Kansas City. Although I was becoming more focused on organic and local production, I never really imagined that I would become a farmer!"

Then she met Hoffman, who at the time was interning with a small urban vegetable farmer. "Sarah really helped bring me closer to the local food movement and helped to define the idea that farming could be a career. And it didn't have to focus on corn or soybeans," Smith says.

Hoffman initially planned to start her own vegetable farm with her husband, but after soil testing the land they'd bought was deemed less than desirable for vegetable production, she bought some sheep instead.

Smith says, "We started brainstorming on how to turn those few hobby sheep into a real working farm. The idea of sheep dairying came from going to a Great Lakes Dairy Sheep Symposium. We came home and began to experiment with milking the few Dorset ewes by hand and making cheese in our kitchens. I quickly learned that I was more interested in the farming side of the operation, and Sarah, coming from a science background, fit the mold as the cheesemaker."

Over the next two years, the pair developed their ideas about the direction of the farm, and Green Dirt Farm began full operation.

For Hoffman, the best part about Green Dirt Farm is that it's a family business. "I am right here on the farm with [my] kids. . . . It is gratifying to have them working with me," she says. "They are actively doing useful and challenging work. A farm is such a wonderful place for kids to learn. They come to know the facts of life, science, animal care, so many aspects of life unfold in front of them. It is a good life." ◆

A selection of sheep-milk cheese highlights the versatility of the milk. Note the blomy and naturally rinded cheese pictured here.
SARA FARRAR

continued from page 73
mother culture requires incubation at proper temperatures, and there is great room for error. So the best type of culture for those making cheese at home is the second type: **simple freeze-dried culture**.

Freeze-dried DVI culture can be added directly to the vat, as opposed to the mother, which must be developed outside the milk first. Freeze-dried DVI culture comes in foil pouches; some are even premeasured. Suppliers of cultures are listed in the resources section at the end of the book. Those suppliers listed are tried and true, offering reliable service and products geared to home production. Starting with the small, premeasured type is perfect; if cheesemaking becomes a passion, then you can purchase larger sizes.

Rennet

Rennet is an enzyme that performs a number of functions, the most apparent being the development of curd. While milk is a liquid, there are solid particles within it, which are the basis of the curd. Curd forms when the water is isolated from the solids in the milk.

Rennet is available in several forms: liquid, tablet, and powder. Liquid rennet is the easiest to use at home. All rennet is derived from several sources, including animal, vegetable, and chemical.

Animal rennet comes from the stomach of a calf or goat kid. The stomach contains rennin, the enzyme that does the work of separating milk solids from water. This type of rennet is obviously not the choice for those who wish to make a vegetarian product. Chymosin is available as a manmade component,

Using Rennet

For homemade cheese, rennet is added in extremely small quantities—drops, not teaspoons. Do not think more is better. This is often where cheesemaking goes wrong!

To add rennet to the ripened milk, place ¼ cup of nonchlorinated water in a cup and then add the drops of rennet to the water. Stir. Then pour this mixture into the ripened milk and stir from the bottom to the top, turning the milk gently. Begin timing and expect the coagulation to take from twenty minutes to twelve hours, depending upon the type of cheese being made. Refer to Chapter 1 to read about when to cut the curd; remember, the clean break is crucial.

and this type of rennet is often chosen for those who wish to avoid the use of the animal rennet.

Vegetable rennet is created from a specific strain of mold, *Mucor meihei*, which also contains chymosin.

Lazy Lady Dairy

Lazy Lady Dairy is perched high upon a Vermont hillside. With its views of a crimson mountain range, it is no wonder owner Laini Fondiller decided upon this spot. It's the

perfect location for goats, for taking in ample sunlight to power solar panels, and for capturing wind for the farm's major power source, the windmill.

"I've been making cheese twenty-six years now," Fondiller says. "I learned with goat's milk. I went to France and needed a job. I was looking for work and found a job making cheese."

When she returned to the States, she knew she wanted to farm. "I didn't have any money to start with. I bought whatever goats I could in the beginning," she says, recalling how she started her farm in 1986. Today, Fondiller milks forty head of registered Alpine goats, twice a day, and moves the goats through her fourteen pastures on a rotational system.

She makes a large variety of cheeses, including bloomy rinds, washed rinds, and natural rind—all aged in her hand-built cellar. The time she spent in France is evident in her French cheese styles and cheesemaking techniques. In addition to the goat-milk cheeses, she makes a mixed-milk variety using local cow milk, and she has recently added a blue cheese to her mix. When the goats are dry, she purchases organic cow milk to make her cheese. Lazy Lady Dairy's current offerings include cheeses named Oh My Heart, Barick Obama, Lady in Blue, Fil-a-Buster, Mulled

Over, and Buck Hill Sunrise. Fondiller's market is largely wholesale in New York, New Jersey, Vermont, New Hampshire, Maine, and Massachusetts, but she still sells at one farmers' market a week.

"We make cheese in small, fifty-gallon batches, five days a week," Fondiller says. "My workweek is usually about sixty-five hours in the cheese room and another twenty-eight hours of barn chores. That's if nothing goes wrong! Most days are thirteen to fourteen hours long. You can't be a social butterfly and get everything done. I like people, but I need only a pinch of human contact to be content. You really have to be comfortable with yourself and enjoy your own company to do this work."

Fondiller's advice to those who want to begin their own dairy?

"Ask yourself, who is your neighbor?" she says. "By this I mean, are you all by yourself, out somewhere that things are going to be difficult to come by? Where is the hay? Where is the vet? Are there small dairy farmers out there willing to lend a hand? Where is it all going to come from to keep the farm running? These practical questions have to be answered. I don't think anyone is prepared for the amount of work involved."

In spite of her success, Fondiller has no plans to expand her cheesemaking operations. "I don't want to get any bigger," she says. "We like to keep things pretty simple here. That's the way I want things to run—simple." ◆

The windmill towers over Lazy Lady Dairy. "The windmill and the solar panels on the house run this whole place. We are totally off the grid," says owner Laini Fondiller. This small cheese plant is a model for those considering alternative energy sources. Batteries store power for later use, and the entire cheese plant, milking operation, aging cellar, and home are run from the two power sources.

Lazy Lady cheese, freshly made from 100 percent organic goat milk. After it is air dried, it will move on to the aging cellar. Cheese is made in small batches at Lazy Lady Dairy, and production takes place five days a week. Saturday is farmers' market day in nearby Montpelier, Vermont.

Mary Keehne, pictured outside the production facility for Cypress Grove chèvre. "I started making cheese in my own kitchen with goat milk and vinegar," Keehne recalls. Amazing where a dream can take you! Keehne is one of the original "California girls" who started making cheese in the 1970s. CYPRESS GROVE

Cypress Grove

When Mary Keehne purchased her first goat many years ago, she could not have imagined where that path would lead.

"When we were living in Sonoma, right after my first daughter was born in 1970, we lived next door to a cow dairy that used the goats for brush control," Keehne recalls. "I . . . wanted good, fresh milk for my daughter, [so] I asked the owner if I could buy one of the goats. She said, 'Honey if you can catch one, you can have it!' So I did."

Keehne began to breed Alpine goats, and as her herd began winning numerous awards, she quickly became recognized as the premier breeder of Alpines in the United States. Surplus milk soon became a challenge, so cheesemaking was a natural pursuit.

Below: The famous Humboldt Fog, Cypress Grove's signature offering. The use of vegetable ash is a French technique adapted by artisan-style cheesemakers. The ash adds a layer of complexity to both the appearance and overall texture of the cheese. This cheese is named for Humboldt County, California, the source of milk for Cypress Grove. CYPRESS GROVE

Right: The well-known Purple Haze from Cypress Grove. Lavender accents goat cheese perfectly, although this aromatic herb isn't used a great deal in cheesemaking in the United States. Truly floral, lavender adds color and texture and creates great visual appeal. CYPRESS GROVE

She had a natural flair for making cheese, coming up with innovative techniques as she was experimenting and learning.

Selling her products proved to be a challenge when Keehne first began making cheese in the 1970s. She knew if she could get people to taste the cheese, most would be enthused, and her vision for this innovative goat business would come to fruition. But she recalls, "It was very difficult to get people to taste the cheese. They had often had other goat cheese that they did not enjoy. I tried to make a blue early on, [but] that was not the time. Fresh cheese was difficult enough to get people to try."

Fresh curd is ladled into chèvre molds. The chèvre is allowed to drain, reducing the volume in the mold to about half. Then the mold is refilled and allowed to drain overnight. The next morning, the cheese will be about half the volume of the mold, as well as creamy and delicious. CYPRESS GROVE

Now, forty years later, it is hard to believe getting people to taste Cypress Grove's creations was ever a problem. In high demand and highly regarded in the cheesemaking world, Keehne's creations, such as Lambchopper, Purple Haze, and Humbolt Fog, have become widely recognized and have numerous awards to their credit. Cypress Grove offers a variety of products, from fresh chèvre and fromage blanc to an aged cheese called Midnight Moon. Lavender, fennel, and vegetable ash have become hallmarks of Keehne's cheeses. There seems to be no end to her creative process, and she recently introduced a new product, Truffle Tremor.

Keehne uses traditional French cheesemaking methods, which include hand ladling curds and draining curds in cloth bags. Her European cheesemaking style is complemented by a California edge, and the combination makes each of her cheeses a distinctively Mary Keehne product.

Cypress Grove contributes to the overall agricultural base in California by purchasing goat milk from local producers. "We implemented a bonus system for our producers several years ago, and since then our milk quality has exceeded Grade A standards," Keehne says.

These goats, enjoying breakfast, soon will produce milk for Cypress Grove products. CYPRESS GROVE

Keehne possesses the skill, the artistry, and the business savvy to remain at the top of the dairy-goat industry in the United States. But she says the key to longevity is her love for cheesemaking, the goats, and the art of creating. When asked what advice she has for those considering a career in cheesemaking, she replies, "Do it because you love it. Find a cheese that is uniquely yours—something there is a real need for. Make it your own." ♦

Farmhouse Cheddar

Cheddar is without a doubt the most recognized cheese in the United States. This is a modified version, suitable for the home cheesemaker.

You may be surprised that this cheese is not colored. While the orange color does not change the flavor, for some, cheddar just isn't cheddar without it. I have had people ask for "yellow cheddar" and tell me it doesn't taste the same if it is not colored. Of course, this is a misconception, but for some, the color is as important as the flavor. So feel free to add annatto if you wish: to add, use at a rate of 23 to 30 drops per gallon (1.0–1.5 ml) for a lightly colored cheese. Increase as desired for intense color.

Farmhouse cheddar is a hard cheese that is a little rustic in appearance, but similar in flavor to traditional cheddar. It's a good choice for the first-time hard cheesemaker; because of a few shortcuts, it won't take as much time to make as a true cheddar. You'll be able to eat it after it is made, and it will also improve with age.

Adding the calcium chloride is optional, but it helps to firm up the curd. I recommend using it if you're working with processed or store-bought milk.

A cheese press provides the means to add pressure to the cheese which will cause it leach out excess whey. Presses can be something as simple as a brick (covered in plastic wrap for cleanliness) or a more complicated affair combining weights and followers to press the cheese in a thorough manner. Presses are available at cheesemaking supply houses.

A follower is used to press cheese in an even manner. A follower can be made from a hard piece of plastic or a wooden disc cut to the same size as the mold.

SPECIAL EQUIPMENT

Cheese press and follower
Cheese mats

INGREDIENTS

3 gallons whole milk (cow or goat milk—or a combination of the two)
1 pint heavy cream (optional)
1½ teaspoons of 30 percent calcium chloride in 2 tablespoons distilled water
¼ teaspoon Mesophilic DVI MA culture
1 teaspoon plus 4 tablespoons noniodized salt
½ rennet tablet dissolved in ¼ cup distilled water

Combine the milk, cream, and diluted calcium chloride in a 16-quart stockpot or double boiler. Slowly heat the mixture to 86°F (30°C), stirring to prevent the milk from scorching. Turn off the heat and add the culture. Mix thoroughly. Cover the pot and allow it to rest at 86°F (30°C) for 1½ hours.

Slowly increase the temperature of the milk to 90°F (32.2°C). Stir 1 teaspoon flaked salt into the rennet solution. Stir this solution gently into the milk. Turn off the heat and let the milk set covered for 1½ hours or until the curd shows a clean break.

Using a long-bladed stainless-steel knife, cut the curd into ½-inch (13-mm) cubes. Indirectly heat the curds to 100°F (37.7°C) by increasing the temperature no faster than two degrees every five minutes. It should take 30 minutes to reach 100°F (37.7°C). Gradually heating the curds is best done in a double boiler or a sink full of 100 to 110°F (37.7 to 43.3°C) water. Stir frequently to prevent the curds forming a mass. Adjust the temperature of your sink water as needed.

Line a colander with cheesecloth and place it in a sink. Pour the curds and whey into the colander and allow the curds to drain. Sprinkle 3 tablespoons of salt over the curds and gently mix it in, using your hands.

Place the curds into the plastic cheese mold lined with cheesecloth. Pull up on the sides of the cloth to avoid any bunching. After pouring all the curds into the mold, lay the excess length of cheesecloth evenly over the top of the curds. Place the follower on top of the curd and set a 4-pound (1.8-kg) weight (such as a container holding a half gallon of water) on top of the follower. Press the cheese for 15 minutes.

Remove the cheese from the press and take it out of the cheesecloth. Place the cheesecloth back in the mold and return the cheese to the mold upside down. Fold the excess cheesecloth over the cheese and again put the follower on top of the cheese. Now press the cheese with 8 pounds (3.6 kg) of pressure for 12 hours.

Remove the cheese from the press as before and unwrap the cloth. Mix 1 tablespoon of salt with ½ cup of water. Using a corner of the cheesecloth, lightly apply this saltwater wash to the cheese. Place the cheese on a bamboo mat to air dry for 1 to 3 days; turn it over twice each day. When it starts to form a yellowish rind and is dry to the touch, it is ready to eat or wax for storage.

Aging Your Cheddar

Cheddar may be aged for weeks, months, or years. The longer it ages, the stronger its flavor and the more dry it becomes. When you are first learning to make cheese, eat it after a few weeks to see if you are on the right track. Once your techniques are established, then you can start to age the cheese out for several months.

Quick Cheddar

Another variation on the classic cheddar.

SPECIAL EQUIPMENT
Cheese press
Cheese mat

INGREDIENTS
1 gallon fresh cow milk
¼ teaspoon Mesophilic DVI MA
  culture
¼ teaspoon liquid rennet dissolved in
  ½ cup nonchlorinated water
1 tablespoon noniodized salt

In a large cooking pot, warm the milk to 90°F (32.2°C). Add the culture and mix thoroughly with a whisk until the culture is uniformly blended into the milk. Allow the milk to ripen for 1 hour.

Slowly add the rennet solution into the milk, stirring constantly with a whisk. Stir for at least 5 minutes. Allow the milk to set for 1 to 2 hours until a firm curd is set and a clean break can be obtained when the curd is cut.

With a long knife, cut the curds into ¼-inch (6.5-mm) cubes. Allow the curds to sit for 15 minutes to firm up.

Slowly raise the temperature of the milk to 102°F (38.8°C); it should take as long as 45 minutes to reach this temperature. During this time, gently stir the curds every few minutes so they don't mat together. Cook the curds at 102°F (38.8°C) for another 45 minutes, stirring gently.

Line a colander with cheesecloth and pour in the mixture to drain off the whey. Pour quickly and do not allow the curds to mat. Place the curds back into the double boiler at 102°F (38.8°C). Stir the curds to separate any particles that have matted. Add the salt and mix thoroughly. Cook the curds for 1 hour, stirring every few minutes.

Carefully place the curds into your cheesecloth-lined mold. Press the cheese with about 20 pounds (9 kg) of pressure for 45 minutes. Remove the cheese from the press and flip it. (If you want to make cheese curds, stop here and go to the following recipe.)

Press the cheese with about 40 pounds (18 kg) of pressure for 3 hours. Remove the cheese from the press and flip it. Press the cheese with about 50 pounds of weight for 24 hours. Remove the cheese from the press.

Place the cheese on a cheese board and dry at room temperature for 3 to 5 days until the cheese is dry to the touch.

Wax the cheese and age it in your refrigerator for 3 to 24 months. The longer the cheese is aged, the sharper the flavor it will develop.

Cheddar Uses and Pairings

— — — — —

Cheddar is versatile: it melts, it grates, and it can't be beat on top of a piece of hot apple pie!

Cheese Curds

If you have ever been to Wisconsin and had fresh cheese curds, you will love these.

Use the "Quick Cheddar" recipe and follow the directions until you reach the notation for curds.

    Press the cheese with about 20 pounds (9 kg) of pressure for 15 minutes.

    Remove the cheese from the mold and cut it into french-fry-like pieces. Toss these pieces gently in a bowl, let them air dry a few minutes, and you have fresh cheddar curds.

Cheese Curds Uses and Pairings

— — — — — —

Squeaky curds are great snacks for little kids—and big kids too, as they pair great with beer! Add some pretzels, and you'll be ready for the big game.

Waxing Cheese

Make sure the cheese has had time to air dry and the surface of the cheese is not damp. The wax will stay on better if the cheese is cold.

    I like to keep a small crockpot slow cooker specifically for waxing. Simply melt the wax in the crockpot. The easiest way to wax is to dip the cheese, coating first one half of the cheese then the other. It is best to do two or three thin layers, rather than one thick layer. If the cheese is too large to fit in the slow cooker, then use a brush to apply the wax to the cheese. Again, two or three light coats.

    The wax can be reused. Save the wax from your cheese, melt it in a double boiler and strain it, to remove any debris left from the prior use. Remember wax is flammable. Use caution when melting over an open flame.

    After waxing the cheese is ready to age.

Goat-Milk Cheddar

INGREDIENTS

1 gallon pasteurized goat milk
¼ teaspoon Mesophilic DVI MA culture
¼ teaspoon liquid rennet dissolved in ½ cup nonchlorinated water
1 tablespoon noniodized salt

In a large cooking pot, warm the milk to 90°F (32.2°C). Add the culture and mix thoroughly with a whisk, until the culture is uniformly blended into the milk. Allow the milk to ripen for 1 hour.

Slowly pour the rennet solution into the milk, stirring constantly with a whisk for at least 5 minutes. Allow the milk to set for 1 to 2 hours until a firm curd is set and a clean break is obtained when the curd is cut.

With a long knife, cut the curds into 1/4-inch (6.5-mm) cubes. Allow the curds to sit for 15 minutes to firm up.

Slowly raise the temperature of the milk to 100°F (37.7°C); it should take as long as 45 minutes to reach temperature. During this time, gently stir the curds every few minutes so they don't mat together. Cook the curds at 100°F (37.7°C) for another 45 minutes, stirring gently.

Line a colander with cheesecloth and pour in the mixture to drain off the whey. Pour quickly and do not allow the curds to mat. Place the curds back into the double boiler at 100°F (37.7°C). Stir the curds to separate any particles that have matted. Add the salt and mix thoroughly.

Cook the curds at 102°F (38.8°C) for 1 hour, stirring every few minutes.

Carefully place the curds into your cheesecloth-lined mold. Press the cheese with about 20 pounds (9 kg) of pressure for 45 minutes. Remove the cheese from the press and flip it. (If you want to make cheese curds, stop here and go to the previous recipe.)

Press the cheese with about 40 pounds (18 kg) of pressure for 3 hours. Remove the cheese from the press and flip it. Press the cheese with about 50 pounds (22.7 kg) of pressure for 24 hours. Remove the cheese from the press.

Place the cheese on a cheese board and dry at room temperature for 3 to 5 days, until the cheese is dry to the touch.

Wax the cheese and age it in your refrigerator for 3 to 24 months. The longer the cheese is aged, the sharper the flavor it will develop. Be sure to flip the cheese every few days.

Twenty-Minute Cheese

SOURCE: This recipe is adapted from Carla Emery's *Encyclopedia of Country Living*

This is a historic recipe, but the principles are timeless. This is a simple cheese; many would refer to it as a farmer cheese. The best things about this type of cheese are that it is quick and easy to make and that it requires little in the way of equipment. For those new to cheesemaking, this is a perfect place to jump in.

Today's cheesemaker would use a plastic cheese basket rather than a traditional cheese basket made of reed.

INGREDIENTS

3 quarts goat milk
¼ teaspoon Mesophilic DVI MA culture
½ teaspoon liquid rennet dissolved in ½ cup nonchlorinated water
noniodized salt to taste (optional)

Heat the milk to 98.6°F (37°C). Sprinkle the culture over the top of the milk and stir gently. Add the rennet to the water and pour into the milk. The milk will thicken almost immediately. Add 1 quart of boiling water and continue to stir gently, separating the curd from the whey and firming the curd so it can be handled at once.

Place a cheese basket in a colander and move the curd into it. When all the curd is in the basket, turn the basket over and dump the curd out into the colander. Then put the curd back in the basket with the bottom side up. The lacings of the basket will mark the cheese on all sides. If an unsalted, uncured cheese is desired, it may be eaten now.

To cure the cheese, leave it in the basket for 48 hours or until it is firm enough to keep its shape. During this time, keep it in the kitchen or any other warm, dry place. Slip it out of the basket twice a day and turn it over.

When the cheese is firm enough, remove it from the basket and keep it on a plate in the kitchen or pantry. Sprinkle dry salt on the side that is up. Using a dry plate, continue to turn over the cheese for the next two days, each time salting the upper surface and the rim. When no more moisture sweats out, it can be placed in a stone crock in your cellar. This would be also an excellent time to wax the cheese, rather than aging it in a stone crock. (See instructions for waxing in the sidebar on page 87.)

The cheese may be eaten at this point or kept for up to a year. It is best when it is about six months old. Age in a cool, dry place.

Twenty-Minute Cheese Uses and Pairings

— — — — —

Eat fresh or age this cheese out—if you can stand to wait! Try this one with fresh pears. It is also perfect on a burger, a pizza, or a salad.

Monterey Jack

Franciscan monks first created this cheese using cow milk in the 1700s. An entrepreneur, David Jacks, entered the picture in the 1800s, believing this cheese to be a marketable product. He began to sell the cheese, which quickly became a popular item.

It is a soft, white cheese with a slight tang to it. Authentic California jack cheese has a tiny eye structure throughout, while jack cheese made elsewhere has no eye structure. It is ready to eat after a month of aging unless you prefer more of an acidic tang, in which case you may age it longer. Jack cheese aged seven to ten months becomes dry and sharp enough to be used grated.

SPECIAL EQUIPMENT
Cheese press
Cheese mat

INGREDIENTS
3 gallons pasteurized whole milk; use cow or goat milk, or a combination
1 pint heavy cream (optional)
1½ teaspoons of 30 percent calcium chloride dissolved in 2 tablespoons
    distilled water (Calcium chloride is used to firm the curd. Use it with
    processed, or store-bought, milk.)
¼ teaspoon Mesophilic DVI MA culture
½ rennet tablet dissolved in ¼ cup distilled water (You may substitute a
    ½ teaspoon of liquid rennet dissolved in ¼ cup nonchlorinated water.)
1 teaspoon plus 3 tablespoons plus 1 tablespoon noniodized salt

Combine milk, cream, and the calcium-chloride solution in a 16-quart stockpot or a double boiler and heat to 88°F (31.1°C). Add the culture. Stir in thoroughly. Allow the milk to ripen for 45 minutes.

While the milk ripens, stir 1 teaspoon flaked salt into the rennet solution.

Increase the temperature of the milk to 90°F (32.2°C). Gently stir the rennet solution into the milk. Allow the milk to set, covered, at 90°F (32.2°C) for 60 minutes or until the milk has set into a firm curd and a clean break can be achieved.

Using a long-bladed stainless-steel knife, cut the curd into ½-inch (13-mm) cubes. Let the curds set for 10 minutes.

Place the cheese pot into a second pot of 100°F (37.7°C) water or in a sink filled with 100°F (37.7°C) water. Indirectly heat the curds to 100°F (37.7°C)

Pepper Jack

For those who like a little zing, add finely minced peppers to your jack cheese.

Add peppers to the Monterey jack at the point noted in the previous recipe. Jalapeño peppers work well, as do sweet peppers.

A note of caution: adding uncooked peppers or ingredients can introduce unwanted bacteria into your cheese and cause food-borne illness. Only use cooked peppers or peppers in a pickling or brine solution.

Monterey Jack Uses and Pairings

- - - - - -

This cheese lends itself well to the addition of condiments, such as prepared horseradish, garlic, sundried tomatoes, and olives. The open structure of the cheese accepts the added flavors, and these flavors permeate the entire cheese. Flavor in every bite!

by increasing the temperature no faster than two degrees every five minutes. It should take 30 minutes to reach temperature. Stir the curds gently but frequently during this cooking period to keep the curd pieces from matting together.

Maintain the curds at 100°F (37.7°C) for an additional 30 minutes, stirring every several minutes to keep the curds from matting. Allow the curds to settle for 5 minutes.

Pour off the whey down to the level of the curd. Maintain a temperature of 100°F (37.7°C) by placing the pot of curd into a 100°F (37.7°C) water bath. Allow the curds to set for 30 minutes, stirring every 5 minutes to prevent matting.

Place a large colander in a sink. Pour the curds and whey into the colander and allow them to drain. Sprinkle 3 tablespoons of salt over the curd and gently mix it in, using your hands.

If you want to experiment with adding peppers, now is the time to mix them in. (See the pepper jack recipe on page 91.)

Place the curds into the plastic cheese mold lined with cheesecloth. Pull up on the sides of the cloth to avoid any bunching.

After pouring the curds into the mold, lay the excess length of cheesecloth evenly over the top of the curds. Place the follower (smooth side down) on top of the curd and set a 4-pound (1.8-kg) weight on top of the follower. (You can use a half gallon of water as the weight.) Press the cheese for 15 minutes.

Remove the cheese from the press and take it out of the cheesecloth. Place the cheesecloth back in the mold and return the cheese to the mold upside down. Fold the excess cheesecloth over the cheese and again put the follower on top of the cheese. Now press the cheese with 8 to 10 pounds (3.6 to 4.5 kg) of pressure for 12 hours. (You can use 1 gallon of water or a 10-pound (4.5-kg) weight plate.)

Remove the cheese from the press and unwrap the cloth. Mix 1 tablespoon of salt with ½ cup of water. Using a corner of the cheesecloth, lightly apply the saltwater wash to the cheese. Place the cheese on a bamboo mat to air dry for 1 to 3 days, turning over twice daily. When it starts to form a yellowish rind and is dry to the touch, it is ready to wax for storage.

Wax the cheese and store for aging at 40°F to 60°F (4.4 to 15.5°C)—55°F (12.7°C) is ideal—for 1 to 4 months. Turn the cheese over daily for the first month and several times a week thereafter.

Mozzarella

SOURCE: David Fankhauser, PhD, professor of biology and chemistry, University of Cincinnati, Clermont College

The original Italian *mozzarella di bufala*, or mozzarella made from water buffalo milk, is a sublime soft, white cheese. Today, it's made from cow milk around the globe, and while the cow-milk version not as phenomenal as the original, it's still a wonder.

Mozzarella is one of the most fun cheeses to make at home. This recipe is for a traditional mozzarella, which takes a bit of time, but it is worth it.

While I was in Israel, I saw this cheese being made commercially. In that setting, stretching machines are used, and the cheese resembles taffy being pulled. The cheesemakers take the cheese off the machine and throw it up into the air, and it wraps around itself on the way down. Poetry in motion!

Cultured buttermilk introduces culture into cheese. Make sure the label says the buttermilk contains live, active cultures. Or make your own buttermilk, as described in Chapter 1.

Note that this cheese requires an overnight ripening time.

INGREDIENTS

1 gallon fresh cow milk
¼ cup cultured buttermilk
½ tablet rennet dissolved in ¼ cup nonchlorinated water
    (You may substitute ¼ teaspoon liquid rennet
    dissolved in ½ cup nonchlorinated water.)
noniodized salt

In a large cooking pot, warm the milk to 95°F (35°C); warm it slowly so it does not burn on the bottom. Blend in the buttermilk thoroughly with a whisk. Let sit 15 minutes to allow the bacteria to wake up.

Stir the rennet solution into the milk, whisking to mix thoroughly. Cover and place in a warm spot. Let sit undisturbed in warm place for approximately 2 to 3 hours until a clean break is achieved. If you disturb the milk during this time, you will have problems getting a clean break.

After 2 hours, test for a clean break. If the curd is not ready to cut, then wait until a clean break is achieved. Cut the curds into ½-inch (13-mm) cubes.

Gently stir up the cut curds with a clean hand. Let sit for 15 minutes, stirring occasionally. Pour off any whey that has come to the surface; there will likely be about a quart.

Warm the curds to 97°F (36°C), stirring gently. Make sure the curds at the bottom of the pan do not get too hot.

Remove the curds from heat and cover. Let the warm curds and remaining whey sit in a warm place overnight, or at least 8 hours. You may choose to place the pot with the curds on top of a slightly warm wood stove, buffering the temperature with a larger pot of water, double-boiler style. Or you may place the curds in front of a refrigerator that blows warm air, but be sure the pot is securely covered.

The next morning, test for a proper spin of the acidified curd by dropping a few pieces of curd into 185°F (85°C) water and stirring it with a fork to see if it "spins" and pulls like taffy. If it breaks apart when you pull it, let the curds sit an additional hour or more until it does spin.

Once the curd spins, warm a ½ gallon fresh water to 185°F (85°C). Pour off all the remaining whey from the curds. (Save a pint of the whey for an acidified brine.) Break the curd mass into small pieces with your hands, using a colander to assist you. Place the broken-up curds in a large cooking pot and pour the hot water over them. The temperature will drop to about 130°F to 140°F (54.4 to 60°C). Stir with a slotted spoon until the curds and water come together to form a gummy mass, pressing and folding with the spoon.

Pinch off fist-sized pieces of the hot, doughlike cheese. Fold the pieces over and over on themselves to form a smooth balls. Briefly replace each ball in the hot water to soften, mold, and even out the smoothness of the ball.

Drop the smoothed ball into ice-cold water to firm up the ball. Repeat the shaping of the balls for the rest of the curd. You should get about four to five 1-ounce (28.3 g) balls from a gallon of milk.

Prepare the brine: in a ½-gallon jar, dissolve ¼ cup salt in 1 pint fresh, cool water and add the pint of whey saved from the curds.

Drop all the cooled mozzarella balls in the brine, cover, and refrigerate.

After 12 to 24 hours, remove the balls from the brine. If you leave the cheese too long in the brine, the surface will soften. Place the ball in sealable bags. Use within several days or a week of preparation. Fresher is better.

Mozzarella Uses and Pairings

Of course, mozzarella is the perfect pizza cheese. The melting qualities are unsurpassed.

And, of course, mozzarella is an essential ingredient in insalata caprese, layered with garden-fresh tomatoes and basil, drizzled with olive oil, and topped with a dash of salt.

Thirty-Minute Mozzarella

SOURCE: Ricki Carroll, New England Cheesemaking Supply

Ricki Carroll is famous for this cheese. It is the perfect cheese to make with beginners or with children. The recipe moves quickly, and the end result is beyond belief. This cheese is best eaten fresh, which is not a problem, because it tastes so good, it won't last long.

Make sure the cow milk you use for this mozzarella is not ultrapasteurized. The protein is denatured in the pasteurization process and will leave you with ricotta rather than mozzarella.

You may use skim milk instead of whole, but the yield will be lower, and the cheese will be drier.

You can add lipase powder to make a stronger-flavored mozzarella. If you add lipase to this cheese, you may have to use a bit more rennet, as lipase makes the cheese softer. Try the recipe without lipase first and experiment later.

INGREDIENTS

1½ teaspoons citric acid

1 gallon pasteurized whole cow milk

¼ to ½ teaspoon lipase powder dissolved in ¼ cup cool water and allowed to sit for 20 minutes (optional)

¼ liquid rennet diluted in ¼ cup cool, nonchlorinated water

1 tablespoon cheese salt

In a large cooking pot, add the citric acid to the milk and mix thoroughly. If using lipase, add it now as well. Heat the mixture slowly to 90°F (32.2°C). The milk will start to curdle.

Remove the pot from the burner, and slowly stir in the rennet solution. Stir for 30 seconds. Cover and leave for 5 minutes.

Check on the curd: it should look like custard, and the whey will be clear. If it's too soft, let it set a few more minutes.

Now cut the curd into 1-inch (2.5-cm) squares with a knife that reaches the bottom of the pot. Place the pot back on the stove and heat to 105°F (40.5°C) while stirring slowly. Take the pot off the burner and continue stirring slowly for 2 to 5 minutes.

Using a slotted spoon, transfer the curd to a colander or bowl. Drain the whey while gently pressing the curd to aid the whey runoff. As the whey drains, the curd will get firmer. Continue separating the curd and notice the color of the whey.

Using a heat-proof bowl, microwave on high for 1 minute, then pour off the additional whey. Knead the curds, and then microwave on high for 30 seconds more until the curd is 135°F (57.2°C)—almost too hot to handle. Microwave again, at 30-second intervals—if needed to reach temperature.

Now the fun begins. Remove the curd from the bowl and knead the curd as you would bread dough, returning it to the microwave if needed. This additional time will allow the curd to be thoroughly heated, so it will stretch. The curds will begin to stretch and stretch some more—this stretching is what makes it mozzarella. Knead the curd back into a big ball until it is smooth and shiny. Add the salt near the finish.

Form it into a ball and drop it into ice water to cool. Refrigerate. The mozzarella is ready to eat when it cools. When the cheese is cold, you can wrap it in plastic wrap, and it will last for several days, but it's best when eaten fresh.

More Mozzarella Uses and Pairings

— — — — — — —

Serve on pizza and pastas, or with fresh tomatoes and basil. Perfection.

Raw-Milk Farm Cheese

SOURCE: This recipe is adapted from Carla Emery's *Encyclopedia of Country Living*

This recipe works well with either goat or cow milk. When using raw milk, 60 days is the minimum time for aging a cheese before consumption, but it's not necessary to use raw milk.

INGREDIENTS
2 gallons whole milk
½ teaspoon Mesophilic DVI MA culture
¼ teaspoon liquid rennet dissolved in ½ cup nonchlorinated water
2 tablespoon noniodized salt (kosher salt is ideal)

Fill a large cooking pot with the milk. Warm the milk to 86°F (30°C). Sprinkle the culture over the milk and mix in, stirring top to bottom.

Add the rennet solution. Let the milk and rennet rest for about 20 minutes, undisturbed. Test for a clean break.

When the clean break is achieved, cut into ½-inch (13-mm) cubes by cutting one way and then the other, to make a pattern of squares on top, and then by reaching in to cut across from the top to the bottom of the pot.

Bathe the curds for 2 minutes by moving them around in the whey gently and slowly with your hands. This helps the curds toughen a bit.

Set your cooking pot in a metal dishpan of water and place the assembly back on the stove. Keep it covered with a cloth. Slowly warm to 102°F (38.8°C), stirring occasionally. Remove the dishpan-and-pot assembly from the heat and let it sit an hour, stirring occasionally and gently.

Line a colander with cheesecloth, fastening the edges down with clothespins if you'd like to hold it in place. Gently ladle the curds into the colander and drain the whey.

Add the salt and mix it into the curd with your hands.

Tie the ends of cheesecloth together to make a bag. Hang it where it can drain. Let drain for about 2 hours in a warm place.

Leaving the curds in the bag, place the bag on a rack, such as a rack used for cooling cookies. On top of the bag, place a plate, then top with a weight, such as a plastic jar filled with water, a brick, or some other heavy object weighing about 5 pounds. Allow to press overnight.

Remove from cheesecloth, and let the cheese air dry for 2 or 3 days, until it forms a rind.

Wax the cheese and store in a cool, dry place for 60 days or more.

Queso Fresco

SOURCE: Inspired by Paula Lambert of the Mozzarella Company

Queso fresco translates to "fresh cheese." In Mexico, this cheese is made of either cow or goat milk. It is the cheese most associated with Mexican cooking. Quick and easy to make, it is a good cheese for beginners.

INGREDIENTS

1 gallon homogenized, pasteurized milk
1 cup yogurt with acidophilus cultures
¼ to ½ cup distilled white vinegar
½ to 1 teaspoon noniodized salt or to taste

Pour the milk into a large cooking pot and stir in the yogurt. Cover the pot and set aside at room temperature for 4 hours.

Remove the pot lid, place the pot over medium heat and bring the mixture to 185°F (85°C), stirring as necessary to keep the milk from scorching on the bottom of the pot. Remove the pot from the heat.

Slowly drizzle ¼ cup vinegar into the mixture, stirring constantly. Continue to add up to ¼ cup more vinegar, until the mixture coagulates into curds. You will recognize a distinct change when the curds form: they will be white and separate from the whey, which will be yellowish in color. You may not need to add all the vinegar. Cover the pot and set aside for 5 to 10 minutes.

Line a colander with cheesecloth or your flour sack dishtowel. Place it in the sink to drain. Pour the curds into the colander. The whey will immediately start to drain. Drain for 10 minutes.

Line two cheese baskets with cheesecloth.

Remove the curds from the colander and place them in a bowl adding salt. Work the salt in with your hands. Add salt to taste.

Fill each mold with the curds and press them slightly into the cheesecloth lined basket. Cover the basket filled with curds with plastic wrap and chill. This is a fresh cheese and will not improve with age, so enjoy it right way. It keeps about a week if refrigerated.

Queso Fresco Uses and Pairings

– – – – –

Nothing can compare to this cheese as a topping for classic Mexican dishes. Try it on handmade tortillas, carne asada, or red beans. Or try queso fresco topped with fresh pico de gallo, or making a quesadilla with this cheese. It's guaranteed to become a favorite.

Manchego

SOURCE: Bob Peak of the Beverage People

Manchego originated in Spain, where it was generally made from goat milk. Traditionally, it was placed in a mold made of hand-plaited strands of a tough grass, called *esparto*, which leaves an imprint on the sides and top of the cheese. Plastic molds have replaced this traditional aging method, but the molds are manufactured to replicate the pattern of the plaited grass. This pattern gives the cheese a rustic and appealing appearance. The rind develops a pleasing buttery flavor as it ages.

In Spain today, various milk combinations are used in its production. Some creameries use sheep milk alone, while others add cow milk or goat milk to a sheep-milk blend. To make it with goat milk, simply adjust the cooking temperature to 100°F (37.7°C). To compensate for the otherwise milder flavor of cow milk, add lipase enzyme.

This recipe makes a small wheel, about 12 ounces (340 g) when complete. Double everything for a larger, 24-ounce (680-g) wheel.

SPECIAL EQUIPMENT
Cheese press

INGREDIENTS
1 gallon whole cow milk

½ teaspoon calcium chloride dissolved in ¼ cup water

¼ teaspoon Mesophilic DVI MA culture and ¼ teaspoon Thermophilic culture dissolved in ¼ cup water

¼ teaspoon lipase powder dissolved in ¼ cup water (let stand 20 minutes)

¼ teaspoon liquid rennet dissolved in ½ cup water

noniodized salt for brine

In a large cooking pot, heat the milk to 86°F (30°C). Add the calcium-chloride solution and stir. Add the cultures solution, stirring gently. Cover the pot and hold at 86°F (30°C) for 45 minutes.

Add the lipase and rennet solutions. Stir gently for one minute. Cover and let set for 30 minutes at 86°F (30°C).

When curd shows a clean break, cut into ½-inch (13-mm) cubes. Cut the curds into rice-size pieces by stirring with a whisk for 30 minutes.

Heat the curds to 104°F (40°C) at a rate of two degrees every five minutes; this will take 45 minutes total. Stir gently with the ladle while heating to keep the curds from matting.

Let the curds settle for 5 minutes, and then pour off the excess whey.

Moisten a piece of nylon netting or cheesecloth large enough to double line your cheese press basket or colander. Wring out the netting or cloth and double line the basket. Ladle the curds into the basket. Fold the netting in on top and press at light pressure (about 15 pounds or 6.8 kg) for 15 minutes.

Remove the cheese from the press, unwrap it, place it back in the basket upside down, and rewrap. Press lightly again for 15 minutes. Repeat rewrapping and press again for 15 minutes. Rewrap and press moderately hard (30 pounds or 13.6 kg) for 6 hours.

Make a saturated brine large enough to hold your cheese. Keep adding salt to water until no more will dissolve—about 1 pound (0.45 kg) of salt for every ½ gallon of water. Unwrap the cheese and float it in the brine for 6 hours at 55°F (12.7°C). Turn it over two or three times during the brining.

Remove the cheese from the brine and pat dry with paper towels or clean cheesecloth.

Place the cheese on an aging mat. Age at 55°F (12.7°C). Turn once per day.

After a week or so, when the surface is dry, rub it with olive oil. (If mold spots appear, scrub them off with a vegetable brush dipped in white vinegar and salt.)

After 30 days or more, you may eat the cheese. To save some of it, cut it into quarters, oil them individually, and wrap them in cheese paper. Refrigerate.

The cheese may be waxed or sealed in a vacuum bag and allowed to age for 1 month or more.

This cheese can be made with raw milk if the cheese is aged for 60 days or more.

Manchego Uses and Pairings

The texture of this cheese is somewhat soft. This cheese goes wonderfully with eggs, working perfectly for omelets and egg casseroles. Try stuffing an Anaheim or poblano pepper with it and then cook the pepper on the grill. The pepper will blacken slightly, and the cheese will become soft. The cheese will enhance the sweet smokiness of the pepper.

CHAPTER 4
Molds, Molds, and Molds

Mold at work:

Camembert cheese with

a white, bloomy rind.

There are three basic types of molds we speak of when making cheese. First, there is a mold used to form the curd. It's usually a food-grade plastic form, perforated to facilitate the draining of the whey from the curd. These molds are available from a number of suppliers and in various styles associated with the size and/or type of cheese desired. It is possible for a beginner to make homemade molds out of yogurt containers or plastic drinking glasses by piercing the plastic with a hot nail or a drill. However, professionally made equipment can be used for years and provides an extra measure of sanitation. Small particles of cheese or milk can be easily left behind in a mold that is not made for use in the cheesemaker's kitchen. The investment of a few dollars is well worth the expense in terms of longevity and safety. (Draining bags for curd are also available through the suppliers listed in the resources section, and directions for making draining bags can be found in Chapter 1.)

The second type of mold is in the form of culture, such as a white mold, *Penicillum candidum*, for bloomy rinds, and a blue mold, *Penicillum roqueforti*, for the creation of a blue cheese. A bloomy rind is a white-mold ripened cheese; it is so named due to the white mold that literally blooms upon the surface of the cheese. The term is used to describe cheeses such as Brie, Camembert, and other white-mold ripened cheeses. There are other molds available; however, for the purposes of this book, these are the two molds of focus, as they're the most common and easiest to use.

The *P. candidum* is the origin of that feltlike covering for the bloomy rinds, a covering that actually consists of thousands of tiny hairlike projectiles. This mold also fosters the mushroomy or fruity flavor associated with the white mold–ripened cheese. All bloomy rinds share a reputation for elegance. Their presence on a cheese plate takes the plate from pleasant to extraordinary. The white mold is an acquired taste, so if you're just getting used to white-molded cheese, start with a lightly aged cheese and work up. If the cheese has an ammonia taste or odor, it is past its prime.

The *P. roqueforti* establishes the blue mold and the piquant flavor associated with blue cheese. With proper aging, both types of cheese, the white molded and blue molded, have the propensity to return to a liquid center. One of the wonders of cheesemaking is taking a liquid (milk), turning it into a solid (cheese), and turning it back into a flowing liquid. Surely alchemy is involved!

A perfect example of valençay. The white mold grows over the layer of charcoal, and the two ingredients complement each other perfectly. Valançay can be made with goat or cow milk. However, the goat milk adds those special notes only found in that type of milk. For a real challenge, try combining goat and cow milk in the same cheese. Fabulous!

The third type of mold is one that is more difficult to deal with. Molds are opportunistic; various molds will attempt to take up residence on the aging cheese or in the aging facility. When aging other cheese—those without the white-mold component—mold will come to reside in the facility and appear on any cheese placed inside it.

For example, when aging a bloomy rind, do not place it near a cheese with no P. candidum added. White and blue molds are aggressive and will migrate to other

continued on page 108

Problem Molds

Who has not lost track of a piece of cheese in the refrigerator and grown a fantastic science experiment? Guilty as charged! Those brightly colored greens and blues are feeding off the proteins in the cheese.

A mucor, or cat-hair mold, is also quite common in the cheesemakers' world. These tiny silia form an undesirable black mold, largely due to conditions that are too damp. Remove any sign of this mold by wiping the cheese with saltwater.

Achieving the proper humidity and temperature conditions for growing desirable molds, but preventing undesirable ones, is a delicate balancing act. This is where the science, the know-how, and the instinct converge, and the true skill of the cheesemaker emerges. Remember, if this were easy, everyone would be making cheese!

The Mozzarella Company

Paula Lambert possesses all the grace and style of a Southern belle. With a Texas accent, a warm personality, and a passion for cheese, she is one of the leading ladies of cheese production in the United States. She is the author of two books: *The Cheese Lover's Cookbook and Guide* (Simon and Schuster, 2000) and *Cheese, Glorious Cheese: More Than 75 Tempting Recipes for Cheese Lovers Everywhere* (Simon and Schuster, 2007).

Lambert's first love is and was mozzarella. "I founded the Mozzarella Company because I could not find fresh mozzarella in Dallas," she says. Lambert and her husband had visited friends in Italy, and knowing of Lambert's love for cheese, her hostess served fresh mozzarella for lunch. As they say, the rest is history. In *The Cheese Lover's Cookbook and Guide*, Lambert writes, "A light bulb went off. I thought I'll create a company and make mozzarella in Dallas."

While her husband returned to Dallas, Lambert stayed on in Italy, sought out a local cheesemaker, and learned to make cheese. After returning home, she engaged an Italian cheese professor to come to the States to assist her in reaching her goals. She researched and found the necessary equipment and milk supply and went about following her dream. That was 1981.

Fast-forward to 2009, and you will find Lambert still happily involved in the cheese industry in the United States. Though mozzarella is still a driving force behind the Mozzarella Company's production, many other fresh and aged products have been added throughout the years: smoked scamorza, goat-milk caciotta, crescenza, fresh cream cheese, ricotta, feta, fromage blanc, blue cheese, crème fraiche, queso blanco and queso fresco, and fresh Texas goat cheese. The Mozzarella Company currently produces thirty-five different types of handcrafted cheese.

Ever the innovator, Lambert continues her research and development of fine-quality dairy productions to this day. She never misses an opportunity to learn. For example, she went to Mexico to learn to make traditional queso Oaxaca.

Paula Lambert of the Mozzarella Company displays her affinity mozzarella. Her ongoing work-study of mozzarella making began after a trip to Italy. "I fell in love with fresh mozzarella, and when I came home to Dallas, I couldn't find that kind of cheese," she says. The skill of the mozzarella maker is legendary in cheesemaking circles. Few dairy products require such skill, manual dexterity, and creative abilities in their production. THE MOZZARELLA COMPANY

"I found the techniques for making the queso fresco were very similar to making mozzarella. It is a form of mozzarella! I was told the people of Oaxaca were taught to make this cheese by a visiting Italian. Of course, this becomes a part of the lore, the story behind the cheese."

Lambert has long made it a practice to employ Hispanic women as a major portion of her staff. Providing needed work and promoting marketable skills among her employees has become as important as the cheese production itself.

"My choice of employees is a factor of where I live," she says "I employ ten to twelve women as cheesemakers, in season. These women have become a part of the company, a part of the cheese. One employee recently celebrated twenty-five years with me, and two others, twenty years. Our employees are the true secret of our company. After that length of time, these people become family. They have raised their families while working here. There is a true history."

When asked to give advice to those who might have an interest in starting a cheesemaking venture, she says, "Be prepared to work ten times harder than you think will be necessary. It is all about attention to detail. First there is the making of the cheese, then there is the marketing, and then there is the business side of the company. There are lots of new companies beginning now. There is a fabulous array of artisan-style products—like never before." Lambert credits a welcoming market and the American Cheese Society with fostering the development of the artisan-cheese industry in the United States.

The Mozzarella Company is one of the most highly awarded cheese-production companies in the United States, having over 100 medals honoring its excellence, quality, and innovation. The first American Cheese Society awards, received in 1985, were first places for fresh mozzarella and a goat-herb log. Since then, the company's cheeses have received awards too numerous to record!

Lambert herself is also highly awarded and respected in the cheese and gourmet-food worlds. She has been listed in "Who's Who in Food and Wine in Texas" and the James Beard Foundation's "Who's Who in Food and Beverage in America," and she is a past president of the International Association of Culinary Professionals. ◆

Paula Lambert ladles curd into basket molds for ricotta. Made from whey, this cheese is light and fresh. The ricotta is a traditional Italian cheese and uses whey reserved from making other cheese. THE MOZZARELLA COMPANY

The bloomy rind covering created by *Penicillum candidum* on this Camembert assists in the overall aging process, adding flavor and certainly complexity. It is hard to believe this creation was once simply milk! Cheesemakers are surely alchemists at heart.

continued from page 105

cheeses. Ideally, there would be three separate aging facilities: one for white-molded cheese, one for blue-molded cheese, and one for cheese without added aromatic molds. Short of that, you can use small, plastic, food-grade boxes, with one type of cheese per box, as small aging chambers within your larger one. Separating your cheeses this way will prevent the contamination of the whole aging unit and of individual cheeses.

Aging in a cryovac bag is a common practice in the cheese industry. If you have a vacuum sealer, you can create mini aging facilities using the same effect. You can age your cheese within these bags in the warmest part of your refrigerator.

Mold can be a cheesemaker's best friend or worst enemy, depending upon the circumstances. Like the t-shirt says, "Mold Happens!"

The Importance of Salt and Brine

While we are speaking of mold, let's talk about salt. Certainly the washed-rind cheese must have come about as the first cheesemakers discovered that saltwater was a convenient way to combat undesirable molds. The first saltwater brine, used day after day, probably developed a certain makeup of its own, and that solution became a part of the cheese. Each day, as the cloth used to wash the cheese was dipped back into the salt brine, little bits of culture, whey, and wild yeast, and mold were continuously reinnoculating that brine. With that unique combination of elements, the brine became a treasure, a secret ingredient, and a necessary part of creating a particular washed-rind cheese.

Salt is an important component in cheesemaking and serves several purposes. First, salt assists in the dehydration process, leeching more moisture from the curds. Second, salt acts as a preservative. Third, it provides some defense against the growth of unwanted surface organisms. Do not use an iodized salt; pure salt is what works best for cheese.

Salt may be added to your cheese in several fashions. It may be added directly to the curd, while it is still in the whey; it can be added to the curd after the whey has been drained; it can be rubbed into the exterior of the cheese to assist in creating a rind; or it can be used in brine.

Brine is another important factor in the cheesemaking process. It improves

The queen of the bloomy rinds, Penicillum candidum produces a covering that has a velvetlike texture.

with age and should be highly valued. Some cheesemakers have a brine that is decades old. Enhanced by the addition of water, whey, and salt, the brine becomes an integral part of the cheese. Whey will continue to leach from the cheeses added to the brine, and the combination of the whey and the cultures in the cheese will allow the brine to develop into a solution that will have its own personality. Using brine is but one way to personalize your cheese and make it your own. Occasionally, the brine will need to have water and salt added to it. The salt will be taken up by the cheese brined in the solution. The saturation point of the brine is perfect when the cheese floats.

How to Make a Saturated Brine

To make a saturated brine, place 2 gallons of tepid water into a shallow container with a lid. Add salt until the water will not absorb any more, and a small layer of salt—about 1 inch (2.5 cm) deep—rests on the bottom of the container.

Place the cheese in the brine. If the cheese floats, then there is sufficient salt. If it does not float, add salt to the water until it does. Allow the cheese to rest in the brine for the amount of time specified in the make procedure.

Brining is a reliable, highly recommended way to salt cheese, because it is predictable in its results.

Cheese aging encrusted in a layer of salt. This photo was taken in Israel, where salty cheese is highly favored. The salt crust is not eaten, but broken away to reveal the cheese inside. The salt layer is added after the cheese has developed a bit of a rind, so that too much salt will not penetrate the body of the cheese.

Pure Luck Farm and Dairy

Pure Luck Farm and Dairy began with eleven acres of land on an old homestead and the dream of the late

Sara Sweetser. She was looking for a place to raise her two young daughters, a garden, and a few animals, especially a little herd of goats.

Along the way, Sweetser married Denny Bolton, and two more daughters eventually joined the happy scene. Sweetser, Bolton, and the girls worked to develop the farm, growing organic cucumbers, cut flowers, and herbs. Sweetser experimented with cheesemaking, and the results became favorite treats for family and friends—so much so that she was motivated to found her own grade-A goat dairy. Sweetser lived to see her dream come to fruition before she passed her legacy on to her daughters.

Amelia Sweethardt followed in her mother's footsteps and began making cheese in 1997. She is now in charge of Pure Luck's cheese-plant operations and manages the goat herd, and she creates award-winning cheese. Her husband, Ben Guyton, is involved making deliveries, organizing the office, managing the company website, and "anything else that pops up!" With a herd of 100 Nubian and Alpine goats to oversee, there is never a dull moment on the farm.

Sweethardt's sister Claire adds her cheesemaking skills to the family endeavor. Another sister, Hope, grew up in the middle of all the action, cutting herbs and milking goats.

"[Hope] gives the best tours and still knows the goats better than anyone else," says Sweethardt. "She always has a smile."

Organic herbs, raised on the farm, happily coexist with the goats and cheese. The fresh herbs are a natural fit with the cheese, adding pungent flavors and a regional flair.

As one takes a closer look at Pure Luck, there is little doubt the operation is less about luck and more about skill and hard work. Sweethardt has a natural talent for bringing out the best in the milk, the goats, and the cheese. The current product line includes Claire de Lune, "a semi-firm, ripened cheese that tastes like Brie, slices like cheddar, and can be grated like parmesan"; Sainte Maure, an authentic French regional cheese; and Del Cielo, a soft, ripened Camembert type.

Since 1997, Pure Luck has found favor in competitions and won awards from the American Cheese Society, taking first place in the blue cheese category with Hopelessly Bleu, one of the company's most popular creations, in 2009. That same year, the basket-molded chèvre won first place in the fresh goat-cheese category. ◆

Caring for goats anywhere in the United States is a challenge. Caring for goats in Maine, known for its long, harsh winters, includes another layer of responsibility

and concern. Fortunately, Caitlin Hunter, the primary cheesemaker at Appleton Creamery, has years of experience caring for her charges: forty-five head of Alpine dairy goats that dot her land and fill her heart.

Hunter says the goats' personalities "range from frustrating, enraging, entertaining to loving," adding, "There is nothing like the unconditional love an animal can give. They are great listeners and never judgmental, always forgiving." The kids are all raised by hand, and every one has a name.

Hunter's love of goats began during the 1970s, "when the back-to-the-land movement first began," and she discovered she loved growing her own food. Raising goats was a part of her efforts. What began as a desire for good food has become a lifelong pursuit. "Those who have had them know [that] once you have goats in your life, it's hard to leave them behind," she says.

Hunter moved to the six-acre farm in Maine when she married her husband, Brad. In addition to goats, the farm also has chickens, an orchard, and a vineyard.

"When you have goats, you start needing income from them to support them, and cheesemaking came naturally to me," Hunter says. "When we decided to build a commercial dairy and cheese plant here, it took us four years to build everything and [get all the] source equipment."

"I can envision myself continuing with the cheesemaking long after the goats are gone," she says. "I got my first goats in 1979, and started making cheese in the kitchen in 1981. I was licensed to make goat cheese in another location (and another life) in the early 1980s, but married Brad and moved to Appleton in 1988. We got state licensing as Appleton Creamery in 1994. I had to give up my goats when I left the previous life, and when I met Brad, he said, 'If you want to have goats again, we'll get goats,' and he's been a full partner ever since. He built all the barns and the dairy for me."

Now, after 31 years in the goat and cheesemaking business, Hunter is beginning to think about retirement. She says she'd like to find a partner who can take over the goats and produce milk, while she continues making cheese. ♦

Caitlin Hunter toils over a vat of curds and whey. When you taste Caitlin's award-winning cheese, you will understand this is a labor of love.

Blue Cheese

This cheese is a simple adaptation of a soft cheese—the molded goat cheese from Chapter 1—inoculated with blue (Penicillum roqueforti) mold. You may use cow milk rather than goat milk for it.

The texture and open structure of the cheese allow the mold to have air to replicate. Putting holes in blue cheese also encourages the molding process. The tracks provide a route for the mold to follow as it replicates. The open structure of the cheese comes from the fact that it is not heavily pressed; therefore a good bit of space remains between the curds. The holes are made with skewers that provide air and also a track for the mold to follow.

SPECIAL EQUIPMENT

Small crottin or open-bottom molds
Skewers

INGREDIENTS

1 gallon pasteurized goat milk
¼ teaspoon Mesophilic DVI MA culture
⅛ teaspoon Penicillum roqueforti
¼ teaspoon liquid rennet diluted in ¼ cup nonchlorinated water
1 tablespoon noniodized salt

Pour the milk into a pot, warm it to 76°F (24.4°C), and then remove from heat. Sprinkle the culture and the Penicillum roqueforti over the top of the milk and gently stir, making sure the culture is dissolved and well integrated into the milk. Allow this mixture to sit for about 45 minutes, so the culture has time to develop.

Next add the rennet solution, stirring gently to distribute it throughout the milk. Let the mixture rest, covered with a cloth for 20 to 30 minutes, until a clean break is achieved.

Once the clean break stage has been achieved, cut the curd into ½-inch (13-mm) pieces. Let the curds rest for 10 minutes.

Work the salt into the curds.

A variety of mold shapes may be used. A small crottin mold will work, as will the open-bottom mold used for camembert. The cheese will turn out differently, depending upon your choice of molds. It is interesting to make the same cheese and place it in different mold formats to see how the shape and size of the cheese affects the end result.

Once you have decided upon the mold size, gently ladle the curds into the molds. Not all of the curds will fit into the molds. (Do not drain the curds in a colander, as other recipes have recommended.) After letting the molds drain for 2 hours, go back and refill them to the top with the remaining curds, and allow them to drain.

In 4 hours, flip the cheese in the molds, so the top is on the bottom. Flip it again 2 hours later, then allow it to drain overnight.

The next morning, remove the cheese from the molds and let air dry. Place the cheese on a mat and let it sit at room temperature for 2 days, turning it throughout this time.

Now things get interesting. Using a skewer, poke holes in the top of the cheese. For a small crottin mold, make 15 holes; for a larger format, make 30 to 40 holes. Place this cheese in your plastic box with a piece of cheese mat in the bottom. Keep the cheese up and out of any whey that continues to drain.

Put the cheese in a cool place—50 to 55°F (10 to 12.7°C).

Check on the cheese every other day. This cheese is a bit tricky; we do not want it to dry out, but at the same time we don't want to encourage any mold other than the blue to procreate. The covered box will help to retain moisture. However, if it appears the cheese is becoming dry, then add a small amount of water to the bottom of the box and then make sure to place the cheese on the mat above the water. Making blue cheese is difficult, so it will take time to learn its peculiarities and specific requirements. It will be worth the effort

After the first week, turn the cheese once a week. Let it age for 8 weeks.

Blue Cheese Uses and Pairings

We see blue cheese used frequently in salad dressings; however, do not judge a blue in that context. Often, lesser-quality blue cheeses are used in salad dressings. Invest in a premium blue, such as a Maytag, and then make your decision as to whether you are a fan of blue cheese or not. For some it takes some time to develop a taste for the blue molds. For others it is heaven on Earth.

Blue should be served on a plate by itself so it will not influence other cheeses. It is the perfect final cheese to serve in a cheese tasting, where cheeses are offered from mildest to strongest. Try this cheese stuffed in a pitted date. The sharp flavor of this cheese combined with the sweetness of the date is an unusual and memorable combination.

Chaource

Chaource is in a class all its own. This bloomy rind originates from the Champagne region of France. It is made of cow milk and is typically a short, squatty cheese. This is another white mold–ripened cheese. It is especially nice when made in the small crottin-type molds.

SPECIAL EQUIPMENT
Crottin molds

INGREDIENTS
1 gallon pasteurized goat or cow milk
¼ teaspoon Mesophilic DVI MA culture
⅛ teaspoon Penicillum candidum
¹⁄₁₆ teaspoon Geotrichum candidum
¼ teaspoon liquid rennet dissolved in ¼ cup nonchlorinated water
noniodized salt for brine

In a large cooking pot, heat the milk to 86°F (30°C). Add the culture, Penicillum candidum, and Geotrichum candidum. Stir thoroughly, top to bottom. Add the rennet solution, stirring top to bottom again. Allow the milk to rest for 30 minutes or until a clean break is achieved.

After a clean break has been achieved, cut the curd into ½-inch (13-mm) cubes. Allow the curds to rest for 5 minutes.

Gently ladle the curds into the small crottin molds. Fill the molds to the top. Allow the whey to drain for about 4 to 6 hours, then refill. Let sit overnight.

The next day, unmold the crottins and let the cheese air dry 4 to 6 hours. Place cheeses in a fully saturated brine for 10 minutes, then remove them and air dry again for 15 minutes.

Place the cheeses in a 50° to 55°F (10 to 12.7°C) environment. Allow white mold to develop for 7 to 10 days or until the cheese is evenly covered with mold. After the mold is fully developed, wrap the cheese in wax paper or cheese paper, and allow it to age for 21 to 30 days. Serve at room temperature.

Chaource Uses and Pairings

Chaource should not be runny; if so, it's probably too ripe. This is another cheese that stands on its own. Pair it with a rosé and little else.

Valençay

Valençay just may be more art than cheese. Valençay originated in a French town of the same name. In France, this fine chèvre is traditionally made with a coating of vegetable ash. This ash consists of burned root vegetables or grape vines. It is thought the practice of using the ash began as a way to disguise some of the mold on cheese, which some people find unattractive. However, the ash also assists in holding moisture in the cheese and changes the cheese's consistency and texture, firming it a bit.

Edible charcoal is the American substitute for vegetable ash. Try making some of the cheeses without the ash or charcoal and making some with. Go ahead and spray the mold solution and then compare. Both versions will be delicious, but you will note a difference.

Valençay is always made in a pyramid-shaped mold.

A refrigerator for chilling wine (a wine cooler) makes an excellent aging environment for this cheese. If you do not have that option, then you can age it in your home refrigerator.

SPECIAL EQUIPMENT
Pyramid-shaped molds
Spray bottle

FOR SPRAY SOLUTION
⅛ teaspoon Penicillum candidum
½ teaspoon sugar
½ teaspoon noniodized salt
⅛ cup nonchlorinated water

INGREDIENTS
1 gallon pasteurized goat or cow milk
⅛ teaspoon Mesophilic DVI MA culture
⅛ teaspoon Penicillum candidum
¼ teaspoon liquid rennet dissolved in ¼ cup cool nonchlorinated water
edible charcoal
noniodized salt for brine

In a large cooking pot, warm the milk to 76°F (24.4°C) and then remove from heat. Sprinkle the culture over the top of the milk; gently stir, making sure the culture is dissolved and well integrated into the milk. Allow this mixture to sit for 45 minutes, so the culture has time to develop.

Add the rennet solution and stir from the bottom of the pot until it is well integrated. Let the milk rest, covered with a cloth. After 20 minutes, test the milk for signs of the clean break.

Once the clean break has been achieved, cut the curd into ½-inch (13-mm) cubes. Allow the curds to rest for 10 minutes.

Fill the molds with the curd, allowing the curd to drain down about half way, then refill so you will have a nice full mold. Allow the cheese to drain overnight.

To remove the cheese from the molds, run a table knife between the edge of the cheese and the mold. Quickly turn the mold upside down and rap it on a hard surface. The cheese will dislodge.

Allow the pyramids to dry on a rack about 4 to 6 hours before placing them in saturated salt brine. Since these cheeses are small, brine them for only 20 minutes. Place the cheeses back on the drying rack and allow them to dry only about 15 minutes.

Coat the cheese with charcoal by shaking the charcoal powder over the cheese to cover it thoroughly.

Prepare the solution to spray on over the ash: mix the ingredients in a spray bottle. Thoroughly spray the solution over the charcoal. Some of the charcoal will run off, which is normal.

Age the cheese at about 50° to 55°F (10 to 12.7°C). You will note white mold development in about 3 days. Let this development continue until it thoroughly covers the cheese, usually in 7 to 10 days. Then wrap the cheese in wax paper or specialty cheese paper and continue to age it at the same temperature for about 21 days. It will be ready to eat at any stage, but will be well ripened at 21 days.

To serve, bring the cheese to room temperature.

Valençay Uses and Pairings

— — — — —

It is difficult to find something this cheese does not pair with. I recently enjoyed a piece of smoked salmon on rustic wheat bread, topped with this cheese. However, I also like this cheese unaccompanied. The flavor is so good, I don't want it to be lost to something else!

My favorite pairing with Valençay? Champagne!

Brie

Sometimes brie is known as the queen of cheese. Brie is one of the classic French cheeses, white mold–ripened and lovely.

I had always been told that brie was one of the most difficult cheeses to make. I suppose after hearing that, the challenge was set to master this cheese. I love to make brie. It is beautiful and challenging, a true cheesemaker's cheese. This recipe works well with either cow or goat milk.

SPECIAL EQUIPMENT
Open-bottom round molds
Cheese mats

INGREDIENTS
1 gallon pasteurized cow or goat milk
¼ teaspoon Mesophilic DVI MA culture
⅛ teaspoon Penicillum candidum
¼ teaspoon liquid rennet dissolved in ¼ cup nonchlorinated water
noniodized salt for brine

In a large cooking pot, heat the milk to 86°F (30°C). Add the culture and Penicillum candidum. Mix in well, stirring top to bottom. Add the rennet solution and stir again, top to bottom. Let sit for 20 to 30 minutes or until a clean break is achieved.

After clean break is achieved, cut the curd into ½-inch (13-mm) pieces. Allow the curd to rest for 10 minutes.

Prepare the molds. The classic format is an open-bottom round mold. If you are using these types of molds, a mat will be required. I use two cookie sheets; I drilled four holes in each cookie sheet, one in each corner. These holes allow the whey to escape. Line the cookie sheet with plastic canvas (used for needlework) or regular cheese mats. Place the mold on top of the mat.

Ladle the curds into the mold, keeping your hand on the mold, until the curd is "seated." If you let go, chances are the curd will seep out, and you will lose the curd. Keeping your hand on the mold for a minute or two will prevent this. Fill each mold half full with curd and go onto the next mold. After you are sure the molds are not going to slide, fill the first mold all the way to the top with curd. Proceed with the next mold. When all the molds are full, place another piece of matting and then another cookie sheet on top of them.

After about 20 minutes, you will flip everything at once. To do this, make sure the cookie sheets are lined up, put your hands on opposite ends, gather your thoughts and quickly flip the whole thing. The cheese will resituate itself in the molds. Flip the whole thing again in another 20 minutes. And then flip it one more time, 20 minutes later. I recommend flipping it over the sink as the first couple of times. You may have trouble—flipping this apparatus is an acquired skill!

Allow the cheese to sit in the molds on the mat overnight.

The next morning, unmold the cheese and let it air dry a few hours. When the cheese is firm, place it in a fully saturated brine for 20 minutes, then air dry again.

Place in a 50° to 55°F (10 to 12.7°C) environment and allow the mold to develop. You will see it starting in 3 to 5 days. Let the mold develop for 7 to 12 days until it entirely covers the cheese. Then wrap the cheese in wax or cheese paper and continue to age it for about 10 more days. It is ready to eat at any point, but will be well developed at 21 days. Serve this cheese at room temperature.

Baked Brie

A favorite dessert for a special occasion is baked brie. I like to serve it with ginger snaps.

INGREDIENTS

1 wheel brie cheese
¼ cup pecans
⅓ cup brown sugar

Place the wheel of brie in a shallow baking dish. Sprinkle brown sugar on top of the cheese and top with pecans. Bake at 350°F (176.6°C) for 12 to 15 minutes. Serve warm.

Saint Paulin

Saint Paulin was originally created by French Trappist monks. This cheese features a washed rind and will develop a reddish cast due to the introduction of bacterium linens.

INGREDIENTS

1 gallon pasteurized goat or cow milk
½ teaspoon Mesophilic DVI MA culture
¼ teaspoon liquid rennet dissolved in ½ cup nonchlorinated water
½ teaspoon bacterium linens
noniodized salt for brine

In a large cooking pot, heat the milk to 90°F (32.2°C). Add the culture and rennet solution, stirring from top to bottom. Let rest for 30 minutes or until a clean break is achieved.

Cut the curd into about ¼-inch (6.5-mm) cubes. Allow the curds to rest for 10 minutes, still in the whey. Place the pan of curds back on the stove and heat to 94°F (34.4°C). Let the curds settle to the bottom of the pot and then drain off 80 percent of the whey, leaving the curds just covered with whey. Now add a gallon of warm (60°F or 15.5°C) water to the pan with the curds. Wash and stir the curds in the water for about 20 minutes.

Line a colander with cheesecloth and ladle the curds into the cloth. Drain for about 15 minutes and then press. In a cheese press, press the cheese for 15 minutes with 10 pounds (4.5 kg) of pressure. Remove cheese from the press and remove cheesecloth. Redress the cheese in cheesecloth and return it to the press, pressing it with 15 pounds (6.8 kg) of pressure for 15 minutes. Remove and redress, then press overnight at 20 pounds (9 kg) of pressure.

The next morning, remove the cheese from the mold and the cheesecloth. Prepare a fully saturated salt brine, and add the bacterium linens to the brine. Place the cheese in the brine for 3 to 4 hours.

After brining, place the cheese on a dry mat and age at 50 to 55°F (10 to 12.7°C). Each day for the next 12 to 14 days, wash the cheese with the brine, allowing it to air dry after each washing. Use a large soft brush to apply the brine. Rub off any undesirable mold with a vinegar-soaked cloth.

After 14 days, stop washing the cheese and allow it to dry thoroughly overnight. Place the cheese in a zip-top bag with most of the air removed and age it for 2 to 4 weeks at 50°F (10°C).

Wax the cheese. Place the cheese in the refrigerator or an aging space with a temperature of about 40°F (4.4°C) for 2 weeks.

Petite Suisse

Petite Suisse translates to "little Swiss," and indeed this is a tiny little tidbit of cheese about 2 inches (5 cm) in diameter. Petite suisse gets its rich flavor from the large amount of cream used to make it. Use pasteurized, but not UHT cream.

I use a plastic disposable cup to make the small molds for these cheeses. Simply pierce the cups in a random pattern with a hot nail. Rinse these homemade molds well and make sure no plastic bits are left behind.

SPECIAL EQUIPMENT
Small molds

INGREDIENTS
½ gallon heavy cream
½ gallon pasteurized whole cow milk
½ teaspoon Mesophilic DVI MA culture
¼ teaspoon liquid rennet dissolved in ¼ cup nonchlorinated water

In a large cooking pan, stir the milk and cream together and heat to 86°F (30°C). Add the culture and let the milk rest for 20 minutes. Add the rennet solution. At 20 minutes, begin to check for clean break.

When a clean break has been achieved, use a wire whisk and break the curd into tiny, rice-size pieces. Allow the curds to rest for 10 minutes.

Line a colander with cheesecloth, and place the curds inside for about 10 minutes to drain the whey.

Scoop the partially drained curds into the molds and allow them to drain for 1 hour. Turn the molds upside down, remove the cheeses, flip them over, and place them back in the molds. Do this again 1 hour later, and then one more time. Allow the cheeses to drain overnight.

This is a fresh cheese, so it can be eaten immediately.

Petite Suisse Uses and Pairings

This bloomy rind is a little treat. It is perfect placed on a cheese plate; your guests can consume each little cheese in a bite or two. Like other bloomy rinds, petite suisse does not require a great deal of accompaniment. Pair with a sparkling wine and a few grapes, if you would like a touch of fruit.

Bûcheron

Bûcheron is an aged chèvre with a white-mold rind. It is a light and delicate goat cheese that originated in the French Loire Valley.

When is it produced in the log format, it may be sliced, and the aging process will be evident. The outer layer will have the mold, then a middle layer will be buttery and soft, and the innermost layer will be softer yet.

This recipe also works well with cow milk.

SPECIAL EQUIPMENT
Small molds
Cheese mats
Cookie sheets

INGREDIENTS
2 gallons goat milk
½ teaspoon Mesophilic DVI MA culture
¼ teaspoon Penicillum candidum
⅛ teaspoon Geotrichum candidum
8 drops liquid rennet dissolved in ½ cup nonchlorinated water
noniodized salt to taste

In a large cooking pot, heat the milk to 86°F (30°C). Add the Penicillum candidum and Geotrichum candidum, stirring until well blended into the milk. Add the rennet solution and stir again, top to bottom. Let the mixture sit overnight.

The next morning, the development of a firm curd should be evident. If it is not, wait a few more hours. When a firm curd is apparent, do not cut it. Rather, ladle the curd into the molds; you won't use all the curd to fill the small molds. After about 4 hours, ladle more curd on top of the first batch, refilling the mold. Let sit overnight, and the cheeses will shrink to about half their original height. Unmold and salt the cheese lightly. Hand salt it or brine it in a fully saturated brine for 10 minutes.

Place a mat on a cookie sheet with holes drilled in the four corners for draining. Lay the cheeses on top of the mat. Reposition them several times during the first day. Place the cheeses in plastic boxes and move them to a ripening area with a temperature of about 55°F (12.7°C). The boxes will help the cheese retain moisture and humidity. They will also keep the mold contained within the box, as this mold is aggressive and will appear on other cheeses in your ripening area if it's allowed to migrate. Allow the white mold to develop for 7 to 10 days, turning the cheeses daily for an even coat.

After the mold evenly covers the cheese, wrap the cheeses in cheese paper or wax paper. Allow to age for another 10 to 12 days in the 55°F (12.7°C) environment. Your cheese is ready to consume at three weeks.

Bûcheron Uses and Pairings

Like all the bloomy rinds, this cheese does not require much in the way of accompaniment. Fresh fruit or a light fruit wine serves merely as an accent.

Bûcheron Variation

For an interesting and lovely variation on this recipe, put a layer of edible charcoal on top of the first curd ladled into the mold, before adding the second layer. This charcoal will create a nice presentation and change the texture of the cheese. Many cheesemakers incorporate this technique to divide the milk—the morning milk from the evening milk, separated by the ash. It's a traditional step in cheesemaking.

Gruyère

SOURCE: Inspired and adapted from the Cheese Forum

Gruyère and other Alpine cheeses are part of a traditional style that also includes Comté, Beaufort, and others. They originate in the mountainous regions of France and Switzerland, where the animals are grazed primarily on their way up to higher altitudes. Due to the animals' more difficult living circumstances, the cheeses produced from their milk tend to be leaner. Often the cheeses are made at mountain-based facilities. And the reason this and other cheeses were originally made in wheels was so the cheesemaker could roll the cheese back down the mountains!

You can make this cheese with raw milk if the cheese is aged 60 days or more.

SPECIAL EQUIPMENT

Small molds

INGREDIENTS

1 gallon cow milk
⅓ cup yogurt with live active cultures
¼ teaspoon liquid rennet dissolved in ¼ cup nonchlorinated water
noniodized salt for brine

The evening before you plan to make your cheese, warm the milk to 68°F (20°C) in a large cooking pot. Thoroughly blend in the yogurt as a bacterial starter. Cover the inoculated milk with a lid. Let sit at room temperature—68°F to 72°F (20 to 22.2°C)— overnight.

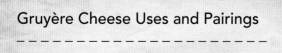

Gruyère Cheese Uses and Pairings

- - - - - - - - - - - - - - - - - - - -

Alpine cheeses are dense, somewhat heavy, dry, and delicious. They are the perfect table cheese, as they will stand up with other foods. Try your Gruyère melted on top of french onion soup.

The next morning, warm the milk up to 86°F (30°C), taking care not to burn it. Add the rennet solution and stir to mix thoroughly. Cover and let sit for about 1 hour. Do not disturb the milk until it has coagulated.

Test for clean break by probing a clean finger into the gelled milk and lifting. If the gel is firm enough to break cleanly as the finger is lifted, go to the next step. If the milk is gelatinous and flows across your finger, let it sit until a clean break is obtained. Do not stir. It may take as long as 1 to 2 hours to achieve a clean break.

Once a clean break has been achieved, cut the curd with a long knife. Begin at the edge of the pot and cut straight down to bottom. Cut repeatedly parallel to the first cut, but increasing the angle of the knife until you reach the other side of the pot. Rotate the pot 90 degrees, and cut as before. Rotate and cut two more times, yielding ½-inch (13-mm) cubes of curd.

Stir the curds for 10 minutes while cutting the larger cubes with a knife. Remove some whey and warm it to 122°F (50°C), Then use the whey to raise the temperature of the curd slowly, at the rate of two degrees every 5 minutes, until the temperature of the curds is 100°F (37.7°C); raising the temperature at this rate will take about 30 minutes. Continue cooking for another 30 minutes, stirring intermittently. While stirring, pick out a few curds in your hand and press them together. When the curds do not stick together, but are firm to the touch, with a rubbery texture, they are ready.

Drain off the whey by pouring the curds into a colander lined with cheesecloth.

Place the curds in the molds. Cover with a piece of cheesecloth. Place the cheese in a press and add a 20-pound (9-kg) weight. After 1 hour of pressing, turn the cheeses over by quickly flipping the cheeses in the molds. Increase the weight to 25 pounds (11.4 kg) and press overnight.

Remove the cheeses from the molds. Place the cheeses in a fully saturated brine for 6 hours. The cheese will take in more salt the longer it stays in the brine. Smaller, 1-pound (453.6-g) cheeses may require a shorter time (6 to 8 hours) to absorb the same amount of salt as a large, 2- to 4-pound (907-g to 1.1-kg) cheese will absorb in 12 hours.

Remove the cheese from the brine. Place the cheese on a wooden shelf in a curing room or cabinet. A cool, clean aging room is important for good-quality cheese. The cheese is turned once every day for the first 4 to 5 days. After 1 week, the cheese may be turned every other day and wiped with brine to remove mold. The shelves should also be thoroughly cleaned with brine and occasionally scrubbed with hot water and allowed to dry before the cheese is replaced. Strive to keep the surface of the cheese as clean as possible. The cheese is usually ripe in 6 to 8 weeks.

Cheese Fondue

Gruyère is perfect for fondue. Add a splash of white wine and melt your cheese. Enjoy with toasted bread.

INGREDIENTS

2 cups Champagne or other sparkling white wine
1 garlic clove
1 pound Gruyère
3 tablespoons flour
1 tablespoons lemon juice
1 tablespoon kirsch (optional)
¼ teaspoon white pepper
Salt to taste
Nutmeg to taste

Rub the inside of the fondue pot with the garlic clove. Add the clove to pot or discard it. In the pot, heat the Champagne and lemon juice on medium-low heat. The liquid should be hot, but not boiling.

In a separate bowl, mix the flour and cheese. Slowly add the cheese mixture to the wine mixture while stirring.

Add the kirsch and remaining ingredients while stirring.

If the fondue is too loose, add more cheese. If the fondue is too stiff, add more wine.

TO DIP

Italian bread, cut into bite-sized cubes
Vegetables, such as broccoli and cauliflower florets,
    pepper strips, mushrooms, and cubed potatoes
Pita or flat breads

CHAPTER 5

Aging Cheese

An aged cheddar:
The aging enhances both the
flavor and texture.

"Age is something that doesn't matter, unless you are a cheese," someone once said. And then age becomes paramount.

Aging is what takes cheese from an agreeable pleasure to an art form. Books have been written about the subject, classes have been given on the topic, and careers have been built simply on the science of aging cheese. Did I say science? Yes—science, art, skill, and tradition are all a vital part of the aging process.

In the United States, much of what we know about aging cheese has come from France. Our masters often go there to learn from their masters. Italy also provides great models for American cheesemakers to follow. So much of the Italian process is about the vessels; the vats, the troughs, and the baskets all add a layer of complexity to the cheesemaking process and establish the specific identity of a particular region.

One cannot discount the heritage of certain foods. Country, region, and terroir all play a role in developing the specific persona of a food. Tradition, too, has played a role in the development of regional foods. Certain foods are only made for specific holidays or special occasions, such as weddings and funerals. In some countries, only women milk the animals and make cheese; in other countries, only men perform these tasks. Specific tools, pots, and vessels become a part of the recipe, and without those implements, the cheese would have pronounced differences.

But offhand mistakes—happy accidents, in which the outcome was at first thought to be an error, but then discovered to be a better product than the one intended—have also undoubtedly made a huge contribution to the development of foods. Aged cheese may have come about in just such an accident. History recounts a tale of a shepherd who forgot his cheese in a cave beside his bread for a few days. When he came back, nature had taken its course, and a blue mold covered the cheese. The combination of the atmosphere of the cave, the active cultures in the cheese, and the yeast in the bread all played roles in creating this new variety of cheese streaked with blue mold.

Recipe Contents

The Science of Aging

Aging is all about time, temperature, and humidity. Maintaining a delicate balance of all three is such a skill that specific schooling exists for the affineur—the person in charge of aging cheese (the affinage), in traditional cheesemaking.

The aging process is what determines the final outcome in the life of cheese. For the fresh creations, it takes a matter of a few days; for a bloomy rind, it takes a few weeks; for a tomme, it takes a few months; for complex development, it takes a few years!

Aging Cheese at Home

For the home cheesemaker, creating an environment in which to age cheese properly can be a bit of a challenge. For those lucky enough to have a cellar without central heat, hooray! All or part of it can be developed into a lovely aging cellar. Think "cave." This space should be well insulated, away from the heat of appliances, and be able to maintain a temperature of about 50°F (10°C). Humid conditions can be augmented or discouraged with the addition of moisture or the removal of it, depending upon the need.

continued on page 134

Cheese aging on boards in a cave.

Morningland Dairy

Jedadiah York mans the vat at Morningland Dairy. Today's make is colby made from cow milk. Morningland has been in business for more than 30 years, creating 100 percent raw-milk cheese.

Morningland Dairy was established over twenty-five years ago. The focus of the operation has always been on producing raw-milk cheese. This was nearly unheard of twenty-five years ago in the whole of the United States, but was especially rare in the heart of the Missouri Ozarks.

Today, Denise and Joe Dixon operate the dairy and create delicious and healthy raw-milk colby and cheddar, which they market under the name of Ozark Hill Farms. The herd of Holstein and Holstein-Jersey cows provides milk for the operation, and goat milk is purchased from local producers.

Denise says, "We are a grass-based dairy and try to stay as natural as possible. We use intensive rotational-grazing methods to best utilize our pastures. . . . [W]e milk about seventy cows every day."

The Missouri Ozarks are known for the natural splendor of their hills, flora, and fauna. The Dixons' grazing system gives their cows steady access to the area's fresh grasses, so the heart of region is present in the milk the Dixons collect and, therefore, also present in their unique cheese.

Following traditional methods for the production of cheddar and colby, the Dixons make their cheese in the cheese house on the farm, five days a week. The cheeses are aged for sixty days or more, then packaged and shipped to its following of loyal customers, which spans the entire United States. ♦

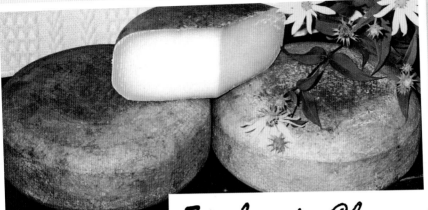

Uplands Cheese Company

When you speak to Mike Gingrich of Uplands Cheese, you will learn about heritage and tradition.

"We make our cheese right on the farm, just minutes after the last cow is milked," he says. "Our cheese is a handcrafted product. We use ancient methods that produce flavor and quality. You will taste the quality of our pasture, our milking techniques, and our passion in each bite of our Pleasant Ridge Reserve."

Gingrich; his wife, Carol; and their partners, Dan and Jeanne Patenaude, began farming together in 1994.

"We joined together to farm more efficiently and to avoid the factory-farm environment, which has become such a part of the dairy industry," Gingrich says. It didn't take long for the partners realized the milk they were producing had unique flavor properties. "The fresh grass, herbs, and wildflowers the cows consumed added a floral bouquet to the milk," he says. "We knew we had to make cheese, and it had to be from this milk."

Having fresh milk, still warm from the cow, allows the cheesemakers to work under premium conditions. Traditional cultures and enzymes are added to create the cheese, and careful aging conditions amplify the qualities of the raw milk, bringing the flavors to life. Complexity develops, and after about four months of daily washing and turning, Pleasant Ridge Reserve is ready to please your palate. The flavor will continue to develop, and Gingrich recommends trying the cheese at a variety of aging stages to taste the various notes.

Present production at Uplands Cheese is 100,000 pounds (45,360 kg) per year. Pleasant Ridge Reserve is an original cheese inspired by Beaufort, a farmstead cheese from the Alpine provinces of southeastern France.

"We found a whole body of cheesemaking knowledge in Europe. We have applied many of the principles to our own cheesemaking techniques," Gingrich says. "There are centuries of knowledge preserved in a wheel of Pleasant Ridge Reserve. ◆

Uplands Cheese Company's Pleasant Ridge Reserve is a Beaufort-style cheese. The production of Beaufort originated in the French Alps.
UPLANDS CHEESE COMPANY

continued from page 131

For the rest of us, there are other ways to create an appropriate aging environment. The first and least desirable is attempting to age cheese in the home refrigerator. This environment is typically too cold and, therefore, does not provide the proper temperatures for aging cheese.

The refrigerators available for wine enthusiasts (a.k.a., wine coolers) provide a workable solution for the aging of cheese. The temperature of these refrigerators is typically warmer than those of the traditional home refrigerator, and the warmer temperatures are perfect for aging cheese. Add a pan of water in the bottom and occasionally spray the interior walls, and the result will be a very adequate aging cooler. Maintaining a temperature of about 50°F (10°C) is the desired goal. Adding a thermometer and a hygrometer (used to monitor humidity) to the interior of the unit will remove the guesswork from the process. Wine refrigerators equipped and maintained this way create a nice environment for aging out the bloomy rinds.

I maintain one wine-cooler unit and age various cheeses in the same environment by placing cheeses in a food-grade plastic box. As described in the previous chapter, these boxes create an individual environment for each product and limit the opportunity for the molds to intermingle or to inhabit the wine-cooling unit itself. Additionally, the enclosed box preserves humidity and assists in the aging process. I've removed the wire shelving from the wine cooler and replaced it with a plastic grid meant for covering florescent lighting, which is available at home stores. I cut the panels so they can slide into the slots that originally held the wire shelving. This type of plastic is washable, and with its open structure, air moves freely about the cheese.

Pressing

Pressing the cheese is an important step in the aging process. If too much whey is retained, the cheese will spoil quickly. A proper cheese press is one piece of equipment to buy or create if one is serious about making cheese. In the beginning, you can press cheese under a homemade weight, such as bricks (before using them, run them through the dishwasher, then wrap in plastic wrap) or a quart jar filled with water. Even heavy books will work. However, if the desire is an attractive, evenly pressed cheese, a press is a necessary tool. Uneven pressing will create a lopsided cheese and, worse than that, leave large amounts of whey in one part of the cheese and not in the other. It won't be long until the cheese starts to deteriorate, all due to improper pressing.

Finishing

Affinage is the term the French use for the finishing of cheese. There are some creameries that do not make their own cheese, but only finish the products others make. These companies receive fresh cheese from various makers, then take charge of the products and finish the aging process in their cellars. This process works well for the cheesemaker who does not have an aging facility and also for the affineur, who gets a finished, saleable product without engaging in the entire cheesemaking process. It's a win-win situation. Some people study years to attain the status of affineur. In France, these finishers are held on high esteem. Together, the proper affiange and the hand of the cheesemaker is a winning combination—one that often produces a winning cheese!

A Dutch cheese press, used daily in a creamery in Israel. A classic style, still quite functional today. Weights are used to achieve the proper pressure, and the wooden followers then apply pressure to the blocks of cheese. An interesting note: It is quite common for creameries to be located in spas in Israel. Whey baths are considered to be healing and luxurious in that country.

Vermont Butter and Cheese

When you love what you are doing, it shows! Both Allison Hooper and her young friend appear to be fulfilling their destiny. VERMONT BUTTER AND CHEESE

Coupole: an American original. Named for its shape, which resembles a snow-covered dome, coupole is shaped by hand and features a sprinkling of vegetable ash. VERMONT BUTTER AND CHEESE

Allison Hooper had direction at age eighteen. As a college student, she spent a semester in France and fell in love. This love was not of the romantic sort, but a love of the French culture, as well as love of goats and cheese. She found work on a goat farm in the French countryside and worked to learn the art of cheesemaking. Upon her return to the United States, she moved to Vermont, largely because of the state's strong dairy industry.

Hooper interned at a Vermont goat farm and also worked at the state dairy lab. There she met Bob Reese, who was in charge of marketing for the Vermont Department of Agriculture. He was in need of goat cheese for a special event, and he knew Hooper had spent time in France. He asked if she could make cheese for him, and she agreed. The cheese was the hit of the evening, and the two realized the potential for a goat enterprise within the state. Soon Vermont Butter and Cheese was a reality.

In the beginning, finances were snug. They pooled their funds together to purchase their first pieces of equipment: a boiler, a pasteurizer, and one vat. Hooper made the cheese, and Reese sold it out of the back of his car. Word of their wonderful cheese quickly spread, and the business soon outgrew the milk house at Hooper's farm. In 2006, they built a new, 4,000-square-foot creamery.

The company began by manufacturing fresh cheese, including fromage blanc, mascarpone, crème fraiche, and quark. Having a product that moved quickly and did not require aging was important to the early business structure. At that time, the company had neither the time to wait for the sale nor the capacity or facilities to age the cheese. The company's fresh products were, and still are, in high demand.

Hooper introduced chevre, feta, and fresh crottin to the Vermont market, and the company's customer base increased. With the addition of the new facility, aged cheeses became a part of the production. The aged offerings include Bijou, a natural, geotrichum-rinded cheese with notes of hazelnut, flowers, citrus, and yeast. Two

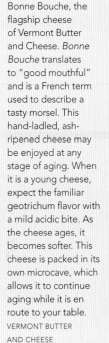

Bonne Bouche, the flagship cheese of Vermont Butter and Cheese. *Bonne Bouche* translates to "good mouthful" and is a French term used to describe a tasty morsel. This hand-ladled, ash-ripened cheese may be enjoyed at any stage of aging. When it is a young cheese, expect the familiar geotrichum flavor with a mild acidic bite. As the cheese ages, it becomes softer. This cheese is packed in its own microcave, which allows it to continue aging while it is en route to your table.
VERMONT BUTTER AND CHEESE

additional aged cheeses, Bonne Bouche and Coupole, were added to the product mix. True to its name, Vermont Butter and Cheese also offers a signature cultured butter.

Hooper's commitment to Vermont, the farmers, and the land remain paramount in her vision for the business. Vermont Butter and Cheese has had an impact upon the local agricultural community. Sustainable agricultural practices and small family farms are the backbone of the business. Hooper's firsthand experience in France taught her the value not only of quality milk, but also of the people behind the animals—the farmers who supply the raw material. She is quick to credit the producers, the farmers, with supplying her with high-quality milk, the basis for all things cheese.

Hooper's creativity is bondless. Her love of cheese and the culinary arts come together in her book, entitled *In a Cheesemaker's Kitchen: Celebrating 25 Years of Artisanal Cheesemaking from Vermont Butter and Cheese Company* (Countryman Press, 2009). This book highlights her years of culinary experience and offers recipes for using cheese through each course of a meal, from appetizers and soups to salads and the main course, and even for dessert. In addition to her own creations, Hooper highlights the work of internationally renowned chefs, featuring their creative use of cheese.

The products of Vermont Butter and Cheese have been highly awarded over the past twenty-five years. In 2008, the company's sea-salt butter received a first-place award from the American Cheese Society, while its feta captured a second-place award. The 2008 New York Fancy Food Show awarded the company its "Outstanding Product Line" award. At the 2007 New York Fancy Food Show, the company's Bonne Bouche was named an outstanding cheese or dairy product. The company's products continue to receive awards and honors from the American Cheese Society. ♦

In the beginning, there was chèvre. Allison Hooper and Bob Reese knew there would be a demand, one day, for goat-milk products. When this photo was taken, goats and goat-milk products were almost unknown in the United States.
VERMONT BUTTER AND CHEESE

Drunken Goat Cheese

Drunken goat cheese is the summation of wine and cheese in a most literal sense. The rind on this cheese is the highlight, as it takes on the deep burgundy hues of the grape. The wine slightly flavors the cheese and gives it the aroma of a well-aged vintage.

INGREDIENTS

1 gallon pasteurized goat milk
¼ teaspoon Mesophilic DVI MA culture
¼ teaspoon liquid rennet diluted in ¼ cup nonchlorinated water
1 tablespoon noniodized salt
Red wine or, even better, wine must leftover from wine making

Warm the milk to 86°F (30°C) and then add the culture. Stir from top to bottom. Add rennet and stir again. Let set for 30 minutes until a clean break is achieved. Cut the curd into 1/2-inch (13-mm) cubes. Pour off 80 percent of the whey, leaving just enough to cover the curds. Add in 1 gallon of water warmed to 80°F (26.6°C). Return the pot to heat, and heat the curds and water to 100°F (37.7°C), stirring frequently to prevent the curd from matting. After the temperature reaches 100°F (37.7°C), turn off the heat and let the curds remain in the water for 1 hour.

Line a colander with cheesecloth and drain the curds from the whey. Add the 1 tablespoon of salt to the curds. Leave the curds in the cloth and press the cheese. Use 20 pounds (9 kg) of pressure for 15 minutes. Then remove the cheese from the press, turn it, redress it, and place it back in the press at 20 pounds (9 kg) of pressure for 30 minutes. Remove the cheese from the press, redress, and press overnight at 20 pounds (9 kg) of pressure.

The next morning, remove the cheese from the press and place it in enough wine (or wine must) to submerge the cheese. Leave it for 2 to 3 days, turning it periodically.

Remove the cheese from the wine and allow it to dry for 6 to 8 hours. Then wax and allow to age in a cool, fairly humid environment (such as a cellar or wine refrigerator). Age for 3 months.

Drunken Goat Cheese Uses and Pairings

This cheese is especially attractive on a cheese plate. The rind adds color to the overall display. Of course, a glass of the wine used in the production of the cheese is the perfect pairing.

Goat Cheese Washed in Beer

The pairing of beer and cheese has recently come into the forefront of culinary exploration. Beer actually is thought to pair better with cheese than wine. While this may seem as blasphemy to some, the proof is in the mug. The microbrews often feature wheat or fruit, such as pumpkin. Those spicy notes perfectly complement the flavor, texture, and saltiness of the cheese. When beer is used as a brine or wash, the cheese picks up the acid and fruity notes present in the beer.

An interesting variation to the drunken goat cheese recipe: Rather than submerge the cheese in wine, wash it daily with a solution of 16 ounces beer with 1 tablespoon of noniodized salt. Wash the cheese every day and place it back on a shelf in a cellar or wine refrigerator. Wash for 14 days, then allow to dry for 6 to 8 hours. The cheese should not be wrapped or waxed, but allowed to age and develop a natural rind for 3 months. If mold develops, wash the cheese with a vinegar-and-water solution.

Goat Cheese Washed in Beer
Uses and Pairings

Try this cheese with your favorite brew. Add a crusty piece of bread and enjoy.

Italian Bag Cheese

SOURCE: Adapted from a recipe by Giuseppe Licitra, Ph.D., Consorzio Ricerca Filira Lattiero-Casearia, Ragusa, Sicily

This simple cheese was probably first made by accident. It is likely the cheesemaker became distracted and left a bag of curd in the whey! Some of the best cheese has been made by accident. This cheese is mild and has a soft, open texture that picks up the salt from the brine in perfect proportion.

This is a fun little cheese to make. It tastes great and will allow you to impress your guests with your cheesemaking abilities!

INGREDIENTS

1 gallon pasteurized goat or cow milk
¼ teaspoon Mesophilic DVI MM culture (Note: MM, not MA)
¼ teaspoon liquid rennet diluted in ¼ cup nonchlorinated water
noniodized salt

Heat milk to 86°F (30°C). Add the culture and rennet solution. Stir in thoroughly. Wait for a clean break, then cut the curd into ½-inch (13-mm) pieces.

Line a colander with cheesecloth and ladle the curds into the cloth. Save the whey in the pot. Gather the corners of the cheesecloth to form a bag and hang to drain for 30 minutes.

After the curds have drained, a ball shape will have formed. Take the ball out of the bag, turn the ball top to bottom to encourage the development of the round shape, and return the ball to the bag. Hang for 1 hour.

Place the curds, still in the bag, back in the pot with the whey. Heat the whey and bring it up to 190°F (87.7°C). Leave the curd bag in the whey and simply turn off the heat. Allow the curds to remain in the whey until it is cool, 4 to 6 hours. Then remove the curd bag and hang it again for several hours until the whey has stopped dripping.

Remove the ball of cheese from the bag and then place the ball in a fully saturated salt brine for 2 hours.

This cheese is wonderful when eaten fresh, just after it's made.

Italian Bag Cheese Uses and Pairings

This cheese is perfect for a tomato, basil, and cheese salad. After the cheese has cooled, slice it into about ¼-inch (6.5-mm) slices. Slice local heirloom tomatoes. Layer the cheese, tomatoes, and fresh basil leaves. Drizzle with olive oil and add a bit of coarse-ground salt. Serve with rustic artisan bread.

Also try warming this cheese slightly, either in the microwave or in the broiler. Serve it with crackers or make a flatbread pizza with it.

Mixed-Milk Cheddar

Mixed-milk cheeses are under appreciated in the United States. Mixing milks is an area of true artistry that allows the cheesemakers to use two or more complementary types of milk in one cheese. Typically goat and cow milk are blended, though sheep milk can be an accent as well. The cheesemaker is able to work with the various flavors and attributes of each milk and highlight them in one piece of cheese.

Mixing milk from varying species can open up a whole new world to the cheesemaker. If you are fortunate enough to have access to cow milk, goat milk, and/or sheep milk, then you can make unique varieties of cheese. You may ask why someone would want to do combine types of milk. There are several reasons:

1. A limited milk supply. If you have animals at the end of their lactation cycles, milk may be in short supply.

2. Goat milk can add value to cow-milk cheese. If you are making a cow-milk cheese and add goat milk, you have immediately raised the bar. Mixed-milk cheeses are specialty products.

3. The variety of cheese that can be made immediately expands when using more than one variety of milk.

There are many cheeses that can be made with the mixed milks: cheddar, colby, gouda, even some of the fresh-cheese varieties. The following recipe has been adapted to use a blend of goat and cow milk. As a rule of thumb, use less goat milk and more cow milk.

SPECIAL EQUIPMENT
Cheese press
Cheese board

INGREDIENTS
1 gallon pasteurized milk
    (3 quarts cow and 1 quart goat)
¼ teaspoon Mesophilic DVI MA culture
¼ teaspoon liquid rennet diluted in
    ½ cup nonchlorinated water
1 tablespoon noniodized salt

Warm the milk to 86°F (30°C). Add the culture and stir in for 1 minute. Allow the milk to ripen for one hour. Add the rennet solution and stir in thoroughly. Allow the milk to set for 1 hour until a clean break is achieved.

When a clean break has been achieved, cut the curd into ¼-inch (6.5-mm) cubes. Allow the curds to rest for 5 minutes.

Slowly raise the temperature of the milk to 100°F (37.7°C). It should take as long as 30 minutes to reach this temperature. During this time, gently stir the curds every few minutes so they don't mat together. Cook the curds at 100°F (37.7°C) for another 30 minutes. Stir the curds infrequently, just enough to keep them from matting.

Remove the curds from heat and, using a slotted spoon, transfer them into a cheesecloth-lined colander. Work the salt into the curds. (Stop here and go to the next recipe if you want to make cheese curds.) Add the salt quickly and then transfer the curds into a mold. Press the cheese with about 20 pounds (9 kg) of pressure for 45 minutes.

Remove the cheese from the press and flip it in the mold. Press the cheese with about 40 pounds (18 kg) of pressure for 3 hours.

Remove the cheese from the press and flip it. Press the cheese with about 50 pounds (22.7 kg) of pressure for 24 hours.

Remove the cheese from the press. Place the cheese on a cheese board and dry at room temperature for 3 to 5 days, until the cheese is dry to the touch.

Wax the cheese and age it for 3 to 24 months. The longer the cheese is aged, the sharper the flavor it will develop. Be sure to flip the cheese every few days.

If you would like to make a raw-milk cheese, do not pasteurize the milk and then age the cheese for 60 days or more. Raw milk is not to be used in the production of fresh curds.

Mixed-Milk Cheese Curds

Use the previous recipe and follow directions until you reach the notation for curds.

Press the cheese with about 20 pounds (9 kg) of pressure for 15 minutes.

Remove the cheese from the press and cut it into french fry–like pieces. Toss these pieces gently in a bowl, let them air dry a few minutes, and you will have fresh cheddar curds.

Stilton

SOURCE: Jack Schmilding

Stilton is a classic blue cheese—creamy, fragrant, with a pleasing acidic bite. Blue cheese is the perfect accompaniment to beef, particularly a steak. Stilton has an open texture that allows for extensive mold development.

Jack Schmilding is the inventor of a great cheese press. You will also find a number of recipes for cheese and his special cheesecake! He says, "It should be noted that stilton is one of the few cheeses that does not suffer from the use of homogenized milk."

Stilton Uses and Pairings

— — — — —

Pair stilton with a robust wine, such as a burgundy or merlot. It is also fabulous with port.

SPECIAL EQUIPMENT

Cheese board
Cheese press
4-inch (10-cm) molds

INGREDIENTS

2 gallons whole homogenized milk
1 pint whipping cream
1 teaspoon calcium chloride
½ teaspoon Mesophilic
    DVI MA culture
⅛ teaspoon Penicillum roqueforti
1 teaspoon rennet
2 tablespoons noniodized salt

In a large pot, heat milk and cream to 88°F (31.1°C). Add the culture, the Penicillum roqueforti, and the rennet and stir for 1 minute. Hold at 88°F (31.1°C) for 90 minutes.

After 90 minutes, very gently cut the curd with a French whisk and let the curds rest for 30 minutes.

Pour off most of the whey, leaving just enough to cover the curds. Let the curds and whey rest for 30 minutes.

Dip or pour the curds into a cheesecloth-lined colander or tub. Form the cheesecloth into a bag and hang it to drain for 15 minutes.

Place the bag of curds between boards and press with 10 pounds (4.5 kg) of pressure for 2 hours.

Return the curds to the kettle and break up them into walnut-sized pieces. Add 2 tablespoons of salt and mix thoroughly.

The mixing of the white and blue molds creates a spectacular range of textures, flavors, colors, and aromas. The white mold develops on the exterior, and the blue more on the interior.

For another variation on this theme, follow the directions for blue cheese with one exception: add an additional mold at the time of culturing. Adding ⅛ teaspoon Penicillum candidum along with the blue mold will produce a cheese known as cambazola. It has a white-mold covering complemented by a blue mold.

For a truly impressive cheese plate, offer a selection of bloomy rinds, blues, and a cambazola. Begin with the mildest brie, go to the cambazola, and end with the strongest blue.

Put curds into a 4-inch (10-cm) mold. Set aside to drain and compress under its own weight. Invert the mold several times a day for several days until the cheese slides out and retains it shape.

To ripen the cheese, place it in a cool and humid environment. A plastic shoebox with the lid on it will maintain about 95 percent humidity with the cheese inside. For the first month or so, it wants to be around 60°F (15.5°C).

After surface bluing is obvious, pierce both ends of the cheese about 20 times with a long needle.

It is delicious at 60 days, but just keeps getting better with time.

CHAPTER 6

Appreciation and Education

A group of artisan cheeses,
including (from rear to front),
a cheshire, Monterey jack,
bûcheron, Gruyère, and crottin.

The pairings of wine and cheese have long been celebrated. Events and blessings center upon the harvest of the grape, the making of the cheese. Indeed, the two are a marvelous combination of food and drink.

Yet there seems to be a bit of mystery surrounding the topic of wine-and-cheese pairing, especially about what cheeses, which wines, and what rules to follow. In times past, wine was all about rules: which wine to serve with which course, which wine to serve with the main course or meat dish. All in all, the rules were a bit confusing and intimidating. Now many chefs have broken the traditional rules and encourage people to drink what they like, with what they like to eat. Doesn't that make good sense?

In general, light cheeses go with light wines; robust cheeses go with full-bodied wines.

While California is most often thought of as wine country, many areas in the United States also offer suitable climatic conditions for growing grapes. Local wines are a great way to bring a touch of regional cuisine to the dinner table. What could be better than locally produced artisan-style bread, cheese, and wine? If it is possible to capture the essence of a particular place, this combination will accomplish that task. Certain vintages bring about the remembrance of a summer's day even in the dead of winter. The robust burgundies or a glass of merlot will warm the soul from the inside out.

In the Midwest, where I live, we have been a bit shy about our cheese and experimentation. I would venture to say the majority of cheese in this area is purchased at a big box store, and cheddar (of a marginal quality) is the most widely used table cheese. Small creameries are working to change that and quite successfully so. Large retailers, such as Whole Foods, have also worked to educate the public about cheese and have had an impact on the development of and appreciation for fine cheese. Smaller wine and cheese shops offer opportunities to sample before buying; sampling is a good idea if you're trying something the first time. Nothing is more disappointing than spending a good bit on something that is not to one's taste. As the old commercial said, "Try it, you'll like it!" You can also ask your local wine merchant or cheese monger to make recommendations for pairing.

A lesser-explored arena is the pairing of cheese with handcrafted beer. Micro-breweries have gained a well-deserved share of the beer market as brew masters create brews previously unheard of. The introduction of fruits, spices, and herbs make for some interesting concoctions. A well-aged cheese, such as Shelburne

Farms' two-year-old cheddar, pairs well with seasonal fruit beers, such as pumpkin ale. Cheddar also brings out the best in honey or wheat beers, such as Hefeweizen.

Blue cheese is sometimes difficult to pair with wines, as it can overpower a beverage and conflict with the tannins present in a full-bodied wine. However, when paired with a bock beer, such as an amberbock or dopplebock, the flavor of the cheese blooms.

Ken and Jenn Muno of Goatsbeard Farm recommend pairing washed-rind cheeses, such as muenster, with an ale. They prefer an aged goat cheese with a lager, and recomment pairing fresh chèvre with a lighter brew, such as a pale ale.

When setting up for an evening of beer and cheese tasting, offer a selection of locally produced beer and artisan-style cheese. Pair those beers and cheeses with similar qualities, such as a light ale with a light cheese. As your palate develops, you can then introduce contrasting, yet complementary elements. Try a stout with a mild cheese or an ale with a cheddar. Offer a flight of three different types of beer with three different types of cheese. Start with the most delicate cheese and work your way up the ladder to the strongest. Enjoy the research!

An Education in Cheese

As interest in artisan cheese production grows, educational opportunities have become more available. As many cheesemakers profiled in this book indicate, cheesemaking instruction has been very difficult to come by until recently.

There is still something to be said for trial and error, for working things out in your own kitchen and coming to your own conclusions. However, understanding the scientific aspects of cheesemaking is important to the overall success and longevity of any cheesemaking venture.

Ricki Carroll: The Cheese Queen

There is one person who stands out as the primary educator of home cheesemakers: Ricki Carroll, the self-professed "Cheese Queen." No one can deny her that title. Carroll's passion and research have led many a first-time cheesemaker down the garden path. With her book *Home Cheese Making* (Storey Books, 2002), Carroll has provided many (including me) with instructions for successful cheesemaking adventures.

"I have been making cheese at home since 1976, when I made my first goat Camembert, modeled after a group on nuns in Canada, and it came out

continued on page 152

Neville McNaughton

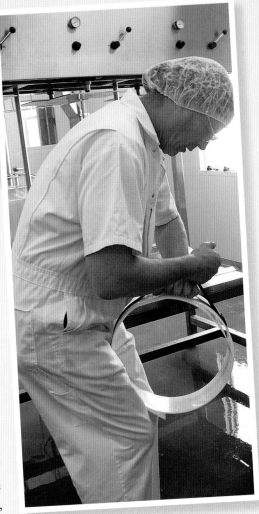

If cheesemakers have a guru, then he goes by the name of Neville McNaughton.

It is not uncommon for McNaughton to pick up his ringing phone and find a distraught cheesemaker on the other end of the line. Failed cheese, wild yeast on a rampage, culture issues, mold growth, and other cheesemaking concerns are all discussed with great regularity. No matter what the question, McNaughton, calling upon his extensive background and knowledge base, almost always has the answer. His problem-solving nature, as well as years of experience, lend themselves well to his consulting firm, CheezSorce, LLC.

McNaughton has been in the dairy industry all his life, growing up on a small dairy farm in New Zealand, where his father milked twenty-seven cows.

"Every Saturday and Sunday, I would go with him to the local co-op cheese factory, where we would take the milk in cans," McNaughton recalls. "My father would ask for a handful of fresh curds, straight from the vat, and we enjoyed them out of our pockets. I liked to go to the back the factory and nail up the wooden crates, which would eventually hold two 80-pound wheels of cheese. It was wonderful, and I loved everything about it. Such was my introduction to the world of cheese."

McNaughton's interest in the dairy industry continued with his first job: washing bottles in a milk-processing plant.

"From there I learned to run the evaporator, then the pasteurizer," he says. "I was promoted and worked in the lab for a year. I completed correspondence coursework to complete my high school education, and then one of the cheese plants in the area paid for my schooling at Massey University."

His path then took him to the New Zealand Cooperative Rennet Company, where he remained for "nine years and a bit."

"All along I was trying to figure out why cheeses are different. I knew the basic answer to that question, but I wanted to know more and come to a true understanding of what makes the difference in each type," he says.

About that same time, a fellow named Ross McCallum was also dreaming of cheese and looking for a partner. Four years later, McCallum and McNaughton opened Kapiti Cheeses, a small specialty cheese plant. The New Zealand cheesemaking community in general, and one cheesemaker in particular, Paul Fitzsimmons, credit McNaughton, McCallum, and Kapiti Cheeses for introducing the concept of artisan cheese production into the countryside. Fitzsimmons says today, "He is the reason we are doing this [making artisan cheese]. He paved the way."

"Our cheese changed the world [as it was in New Zealand]," McNaughton acknowledges. "We introduced funny looking little cheeses with weird regional names. It worked."

In 1986, McNaughton made his way to the United States as a representative for New Zealand Dairy Board, a position he held until 1994. For a time he worked at Marin French Cheese in Petaluma, California. Eventually, he moved to Missouri and worked for Imperial Biotechnology (IBT) for four years. He then went on to work for a company that sold ingredients to the food industry.

At the same time, McNaughton began to work with a new segment of industry in the United States, the artisan cheesemaker, applying his expertise to small-scale production and leading newcomers through the maze of requirements, regulations, and technical aspects of cheesemaking. Since then, his name has become synonymous with artisan cheese.

"Artisan scale is about people—a small group of people doing the work, making cheese by hand," he says. "You don't need plastic bags and vacuum equipment to make artisan cheese. You don't make artisan cheese in forty-pound blocks. It is individual and handmade."

McNaughton's experiences within the industry provide invaluable insight and guidance to those wanting a better understanding of all that goes in to a creamery, from the animal to the milk to the finished product.

"I consider myself a cheesemaker's cheesemaker," he says. "Natural cheeses are the gift cheesemakers have to share, and it is my privilege to work alongside some of the country's best." ♦

Ricki Carroll of New England Cheesemaking Supply at work.

continued from page 149

perfect," Carroll says. "It was like tasting a sweet little bit of heaven!"

Since then, she developed recipes for the home dairy enthusiast. What keeps her going over thirty-five years later?

"It is the cheesemakers who are my inspiration, the ones out in the trenches daily," she says. "The appreciation and connection of humankind is enough to keep me going for many years. I have [also] watched the American Cheese Society over the years. Knowing my role in the early years in keeping it alive has always warmed my heart."

For those interested in cheesemaking as a vocation, she offers this advice: "Go slow, be consistent, and check to see what is needed locally. Get feedback from others."

The American Cheese Society

The American Cheese Society (ACS) was founded in 1983 by Dr. Frank Kosikowski of Cornell University as a national grassroots organization for cheese appreciation and for home- and farm-based cheesemaking. The first annual meeting was held in 1983 at Cornell, with 150 in attendance. The first competition was held in 1985 at the third annual conference. Thirty cheesemakers entered a total of eighty-nine cheeses in seven categories. At the first annual convergence, there were 170 entries in the competition, but the struggling organization was having a difficult time finding its audience. By 1990, a new awareness began to grow, and in 2000, restructuring of the organization provided the perfect platform for growth. In 2009, the ACS had more than 1,200 members, and competition entries totaled 1,327. A medal from the ACS offers untold opportunities for cheesemakers. An ACS award is equivalent to an Academy Award in the cheesemaking world!

The American Cheese Society is a driving force behind legislation on raw-milk cheeses and the continued education of those who appreciate, consume, and make cheese in the United States. A dedicated staff and board keep this organization focused and forward thinking. For more information, contact the ACS via its website, www.cheesesociety.org.

Cheese College

Several institutions of higher learning have dedicated themselves to the education of professional cheesemakers.

The Vermont Institute of Artisan Cheese (VIAC) was formed in as "the nation's first and only comprehensive center devoted to artisan cheese." The institute is located at the University of Vermont in Burlington. Extensive coursework is designed to immerse the student in the world of cheesemaking and covers such topics as the essential principles and practices in cheesemaking, hygiene and food safety in cheesemaking, milk chemistry, cheese chemistry, and the evaluation of starter cultures. Advanced courses include international-artisan practices, advanced sensory evaluation of cheese, cheese defects, risk-reduction practices for cheesemakers, and affiange.

The institute frequently hosts international cheese experts, who offer classes for students and opportunities for the general public to learn more about topics ranging from cheese tasting to international cheesemaking practices. The noted VIAC facility and staff includes Paul Kindstedt, Ph.D., author of *American Farmstead Cheese* (Chelsea Green, 2005); Catherine Donnelly, Ph.D.; Monserrat Almena-Aliste, Ph.D.; Jody Farnham, program director; Marc Druart, cheese technician; Todd Prichard, Ph.D.; D. J. D'Amico, Ph.D.; and Jeff Roberts, principle consultant and author of the *Atlas of American Artisan Cheese* (Chelsea Green, 2007).

Washington State University also offers a cheesemaking short course designed for "experienced cheesemakers, supervisory, management personnel from commercial/industrial plants." A beginner's cheesemaking course is also available.

Wisconsin often comes to mind when considering cheese and educational opportunities. The University of Wisconsin at River Falls offers a four-day short course "designed for the farmstead cheesemaker as well as apprentice cheesemakers from the industry. Sessions focus on the basic steps in cheese manufacture and provide opportunities to gain 'hands-on' experience in the cheesemaking process." Topics include milk composition, cheesemaking principles, milk microbiology, pasteurization, regulations, basic analysis, milk and cheese analysis, coagulants, cheese defects, cultures, cleaning and sanitation, and basic cheese labeling requirements. Reann May, M.S., is the program coordinator.

Cheese Guilds

As the artisan-cheese movement continues to sweep the United States, cheese guilds have been established in several states. These guilds provide continued education for the artisans and a network of support. See the resources section for a list of active guilds.

Shelburne Farms

The famous herd of Brown Swiss cows at Shelburne Farms. This breed is known for its hardiness, foraging ability, longevity, and gentle temperament. This herd provides the high-quality milk in the production of Shelburne Farms' award-winning cheese. SHELBURNE FARMS

This photo illustrates the statement "Cheddar is a verb." This stacking process is known as cheddaring, a term that is the basis for the name of America's most popular cheese. SHELBURNE FARMS

Shelburne Farms is a 1,400-acre working farm, a National Historic Landmark, and a nonprofit environmental education center located in Shelburne, Vermont. The farm was created as a model agricultural estate in 1886 by William Seward and Lila Vanderbilt Webb. In 1972, it became an educational nonprofit. Four hundred acres of woodlands have been "green certified" by the Forest Stewardship Council. The grass-based dairy is one of the examples of sustainable agriculture on the farm, whose mission is to cultivate a sustainability ethic.

The pasture-based operation consists of a rotational grazing system, in which the cows are rotated to a new paddock every twelve to twenty-four hours. The grazed area is then given time to regrow before the cows are grazed on that pasture again. No herbicides or pesticides are used on the land; less machinery and fuel is used to plant, harvest, and transport grain than on typical farms. Manure left on the pastures serves as natural fertilizer, and thick pasture growth means less water pollution.

The Brown Swiss herd is the pride of the farm. This dairy-cow breed, selected for the farm by Derick Webb in the 1950s, is known for its hardiness, foraging ability, longevity, and gentle temperament. The high quality of its milk sets the stage for the cheesemaking, which is a part of farm life at Shelburne. Highly regarded and awarded, Shelburne Farms' cheddar is well known. Made from raw milk, cheese is produced daily from March to mid-November. Shelburne Farms produces about 140,000 pounds (63,500 kg) of artisanal cheddar per year. In 2009, the American Cheese Society named Shelburne Farms' cheeses Best Cow's Milk Cheddar Aged Less Than One Year, Best Smoked Cheddar, and Best Plain Cheese Spread. ♦

Peter Dixon

Several cheesemakers interviewed for this book credit Peter Dixon with their beginnings. Dixon's company, Dairy Foods Consulting, helps new and established cheesemakers fine-tune their operations. Dixon's rich background includes ownership in the Guiliford Cheese Company; cheesemaking at the renowned Shelburne Farms creamery; cheesemaking at Vermont Butter and Cheese, where he was also quality-control manager; and part ownership of Westminster Dairy.

Dixon has also served as a dairy foods specialist for Land O'Lakes International Development Division, Macedonia and Albania, and the U.S. Department of Agriculture Marketing Assistance Project in Armenia. Since 1996, he has been operating Dairy Foods Consulting for clients in the United States. He has been an integral part of noted creameries, assisting with product development, construction of aging facilities, startups, and troubleshooting. He also creates business plans, locates new and used equipment for his clients, and offers workshops to beginning and advanced cheesemakers.

Dixon has been making cheese for the past three years at Consider Bardwell Farm in West Pawlet, Vermont. He conducts hands-on cheesemaking classes at the farm for groups of up to eight people. These classes are generally held in the winter/spring and in the fall. ♦

Peter Dixon shows that cheesemaking is not for the faint of heart or those with lack of muscles! Farmstead cheesemakers play a lot of roles in a day's time—everything from milker to veterinarian to gourmet. Multitaskers, join in!
CONSIDER BARDWELL

As we come to a close, I would like to thank all those who have allowed me to cite their work in this book. I have been collecting these recipes for a number of years now and feel they are some of the best for making cheese at home. Many of the experts mentioned have been my mentors and teachers, and are now friends. As with any craft, time is the best instructor. Have fun with your cheesemaking adventures and learning new skills along the way. Experiment and enjoy!

"My sheep know my voice. Blessed are the cheesemakers."

RESOURCES

Websites

A Campaign for Real Milk (www.realmilk.com)
Farm sources where you can purchase milk directly.

American Dairy Goat Association (www.adga.org)

American Livestock Breeds Conservancy (www.albc-usa.org)

Fias Co Farm (www.fiascofarm.com)
A wealth of information on goats and cheese-making.

Janet Hurst (www.cheesewriter.com)
Information on my projects, cheesemaking classes, blogs, and more.

Local Harvest (www.localharvest.org)
Sources from which to purchase milk, cheese, and other farm offerings.

SmallDairy.com (www.smalldairy.com)
A great resource for those interested in small dairies and in milk and cheese production.

Magazines

Countryside (www.countryside.com)
A homesteader's delight.

Culture (www.culturecheesemag.com)
A magazine made for cheese lovers everywhere.

Dairy Goat Journal (www.dairygoatjournal.com)
A great resource for new or seasoned goat lovers.

Hobby Farms (www.hobbyfarms.com)
Wonderful, detailed information on getting started on your own farming venture.

Mary Jane's Farm (www.maryjanesfarm.com)
A farm girl after my own heart.

Mother Earth News
(www.motherearthnew.com)
The one and only original.

Sheep! (www.sheepmagazine.com)
By the publishers of the *Dairy Goat Journal* and *Countryside*, this magazine offers a wealth of information for sheep people.

The Small Farmer's Journal
(www.smallfarmersjournal.com)
All about draft animals and traditional farm life.

Small Farm Today (www.smallfarmtoday.com)
A Missouri-based publication with great information on traditional and alternative farming.

Books

Carroll, Ricki. *Home Cheese Making*. North Adams, MA: Storey Books, 2002.

Chadwick, Janet. *How to Live on Almost Nothing and Have Plenty*. New York: Alfred A. Knopf, 1982. (Author's note: This book is out of print but worth finding. Depending upon the day, I credit or blame this book for my homesteading adventures.)

Jenkins, Steve. *A Cheese Primer*. New York: Workman Publishing, 1996.

Emery, Carla. *The Encyclopedia of Country Living*. Seattle: Sasquatch Books, 1994.

Hooper, Allison. *In a Cheesemaker's Kitchen: Celebrating 25 Years of Artisanal Cheesemaking from Vermont Butter and Cheese Company*. Woodstock, VT: Countryman Press, 2009.

Kinstedt, Paul. *American Farmstead Cheese*. White River Junction, VT: Chelsea Green, 2005.

Lambert, Paula. *Cheese, Glorious Cheese*. New York: Simon and Schuster, 2007.

———. *The Cheese Lover's Cookbook and Guide*. New York: Simon and Schuster, 2000.

Morris, Margaret. *The Cheesemaker's Manual*. Lancaster, ON, Canada: Glengarry Cheesemaking and Dairy Supply, 2005.

Roberts, Jeff. *The Encyclopedia of American Cheese*. White River Junction, VT: Chelsea Green, 2007.

Toth, Mary Jane. *Goats Produce, Too*. Vol. III. N.p.: n.p., 2007. (This self-published book is available through the cheesemaking supply sources listed.)

Werlin, Laura. *The All American Cheese and Wine Book*. 2003.

———. *Cheese Essentials*. 2007.

———. *The New American Cheese*. 2000.

Tweksbury, Henry. *The Cheeses of Vermont*. Woodstock, VT: The Countryman Press, 2002.

Supplies

New England Cheesemaking Supply
Ricki Carroll
www.cheesemaking.com
P.O. Box 85
Ashfield MA 01330
413-628-3808
Fax: 413-628-4061
E-mail: info@cheesemaking.com

Dairy Connection
Cultures, molds, equipment
Jeff Meier or Cathy Potter
www.dairyconnection.com
501 Tasman Street, Suite B
Madison, WI 53714
608-242-9030
Fax: 608-242-9036

Glengarry Cheesemaking and Dairy Supply
Margaret Morris
www.glengarrycheesemaking.on.ca
1-888-816-0903 or 613-347-1141
Canada: P.O. Box 190, #5926 County Road 34,
Lancaster, Ontario K0C 1N0, Canada
USA: P.O. Box 92, Massena, NY 13662, USA

Caprine Supply
Dairy-goat supplies, cheesemaking supplies
www.caprinesupply.com
P.O. Box Y
Desoto, KS 66018
Order line: 1-800-646-7736
E-mail: info@caprinesupply.com

Leeners
Supplies for just about everything required
to make fermented beverages and foods—
everything from sake to sausage, wine, beer,
and cheese!
www.leeners.com
9293 Olde Eight Road
Northfield, OH 66018
1-800-543-3697

Hoeggers Goat Supply
Cheesemaking and goat supplies
www.hoeggergoatsupply.com
160 Providence Road
Fayetteville, GA 30215
1-800-221-4628

Lehman's
www.Lehmans.com
#1 Lehman's Circle
Kidron, OH 44636
1-888-438-5346

Jack Schmidling
Cheese presses
http://schmidling.com/cres.htm
18016 Church Road
Marengo, IL 60152

Other Resources

American Cheese Society
Find cheesemakers in your area, guild listings,
education, and more.
www.cheesesociety.org
455 South Fourth Street
Suite 650
Louisville, KY 40202
502-574-9950

Vermont Institute of Artisan Cheese
www.uvm.edu/viac/
University of Vermont
Burlington, VT 05403
802-656-8300

**California Polytechnic State University
(Cal Poly)** dsci@calpoly.edu

Washington State University
www.wsu.edu/creamery/shortcourseinfo.htm
WSU Creamery
P.O. Box 641122
Washington State University
Pullman WA 99164-1122
800-457-5442

University of Wisconsin, River Falls
www.uwrf.edu
University of Wisconsin–River Falls
410 S. Third Street
River Falls WI 54022-5001
715-425-3911

Cheese Guilds

Big River Dairy Artisans Guild,
www.dairyartisansguild.org
Midwest encompassing the Mississippi
and Missouri River Valley Regions

California www.cacheeseguild.org

Oregon www.oregoncheeseguild.org

Maine www.mainecheeseguild.org

New York www.nyfarmcheese.org

New Hampshire www.nhdairypromo.org

Pacific Northwest Cheese Project
www.pnwcheese.typepad.com

Pennsylvania www.pacheese.org

Southern Cheesemakers
www.southerncheese.com

Texas Cheesemakers Guide
slowfooddallas.com

Washington www.wacheese.com

Wisconsin Specialty Cheese Institute
www.wisspecialcheese.org

Vermont Cheese Council www.vtcheese.com

Profiled Cheesemakers and Creameries

Appleton Creamery
Caitlin Hunter
Appleton, Maine
www.appletoncreamery.com

Baetje Farm
Steve and Veronica Baetje
Bloomsdale, Missouri
www.baetjefarms.com

Cypress Grove
Mary Keehne
Arcata, California
www.cypressgrove.com

Peter Dixon
Dairy Foods Consulting
www.dairyfoodsconsulting.com

Does' Leap
Kristan Doolan and George VanVlaanderen
East Fairfield, Vermont
www.doesleap.com

Goatsbeard Farm
Ken and Jenn Muno
Harrisburg, Missouri
www.goatsbeardfarm.com

Green Dirt Farm
Sarah Hoffman and Jacque Smith
Near Kansas City, Missouri
www.greendirtfarm.com

Lazy Lady Dairy
Laini Fondiller
Westfield, Vermont
E-mail: laini@sover.net

Neville McNaughton
Cheezsorce, LLC
www.cheezesorce.com

Morningland Dairy
Denise and Joe Dixon
Mountain View, Missouri
www.morninglanddairy.com

The Mozzarella Company
Paula Lambert
Dallas, Texas
www.mozzco.com

Pure Luck Farm and Dairy
Amelia Sweethardt and Ben Guyton
Dripping Springs, Texas
www.purelucktexas.com

Redwood Hill Farm and Creamery
Jennifer Bice
Sebastopol, California
www.redwoodhill.com

Shelburne Farms
Shelburne, Vermont
www.shelburnefarms.org

Tasha Tudor
Marlboro, Vermont
www.tashatudorandfamily.com

Uplands Cheese Company
Mike and Carol Gingrich,
Dan and Jeanne Patenaude
Dodgeville, Wisconsin
www.uplandscheese.com

Vermont Butter and Cheese
Allison Hooper and Bob Reese
Websterville, Vermont
www.vermontcreamery.com

Vermont Shepherd
David and Yesenia Ielpi Major
Putney, Vermont
www.vermontshepherd.com

INDEX